Hard Times in Oklahoma

Hard Times in Oklahoma:

The Depression Years

Edited By

Kenneth E. Hendrickson, Jr.

Bob L. Blackburn
Series Editor

Oklahoma Historical Society
Oklahoma City, Oklahoma
1983

Library of Congress Catalog Number: 83-060262

Hendrickson, Kenneth E., Jr.
Hard Times in Oklahoma:
The Depression Years
(The Oklahoma Series)

1. Oklahoma—History. 2. Oklahoma—Political History. 3. Oklahoma—Great Depression. 4. Great Depression—Oklahoma. I. Title. II. Series.

ISBN 0-941498-32-8
ISBN 0-941498-33-6 (pbk.)

For Emily

Contents

Contributors

D. Clayton Brown is Associate Professor of History at Texas Christian University. He is the author of *Electricity Comes to the Farm: The Fight for REA* (Greenwood Press, 1980), and numerous articles in such journals as *Agricultural History* and *Southwestern Historical Quarterly*. He received the H. Bailey Carrol Award from *SHQ* for the best article of 1975.

Danney Goble teaches at Tulsa Junior College. He has received research grants from the American Council of Learned Societies and the National Endowment for the Humanities. He is author of several articles and co-author with James R. Scales of a book entitled *Progressive Oklahoma: The Making of a New Kind of State* (University of Oklahoma Press, 1980) and *Oklahoma Politics: A History* (University of Oklahoma Press, 1982).

Kenneth E. Hendrickson, Jr. is Professor and Head of the Department of History at Midwestern State University. He has authored or contributed to seven books including *The Waters of the Brazos: A History of the Brazos River Authority* (Texian Press, 1980), and has published numerous articles in such journals as *Labor History, Pacific Historical Review, New York History* and *South Dakota History*. He was named Hardin Professor of the year at Midwestern State in 1974 and has twice been awarded the Karl E. Mundt Memorial Prize for excellence by the Dakota History Conference.

Donovan L. Hofsommer lives in Plainview, Texas. He is an authority on the history of railroading in the West, the author of two books including *Katy Northwest* (Pruett Publishing, 1976), and presently serves as editor for the *Lexington Newsletter*, journal of the Lexington Group in transportation history.

C. Roger Lambert is Professor of History at Arkansas State University in Jonesboro, Arkansas. He is a specialist in the field of agricultural history and has published numerous articles in such journals as *Agricultural History, Arizona and the West,* and *Annals of Iowa.*

Patrick McGinnis is Professor of History at Central State University at Edmond, Oklahoma. He is a specialist in twentieth century political history and is currently writing a book entitled *Depression Politics in Oklahoma: Ira M. Finley and the VIA.*

Forrest D. Monahan, Jr. was Professor of History at Midwestern State University. He died unexpectedly while this book was in press. He was an authority on the Plains Indians, and at the time of his death was working on a book to be entitled *The Kiowa.*

Kenneth R. Philp is Professor of History at the University of Texas at Arlington. He is the author of *John Collier's Crusade for Indian Reform, 1920—1954* (University of Arizona Press, 1977), and numerous articles appearing in such journals as *Arizona and the West* and *Pacific Historical Review.*

James R. Scales is President of Wake Forest University. He is the author of many works including *Progressive Oklahoma: The Making of a New Kind of State* and *Okla homa Politics: A History* which he co-authored with Danney Goble.

Donald W. Whisenhunt is Professor of History at the University of Texas at Tyler. He is the author or editor of nine books including *The Depression in the Southwest* (Kennikat Press, 1980), and many articles appearing in such journals as *Southwest Review, Texana* and *Red River Valley Historical Review.*

Preface and Acknowledgments

Although possessed of a colorful past deeply marked by American culture and lore, Oklahoma had nevertheless been a state for only twenty-two years when the Great Depression struck. Financial and governmental institutions were still immature and ill-prepared to handle a calamity of such magnitude. Despite these shortcomings, there was no alternative but to make the attempt.

The essays in this volume are designed to capture the essence of dustbowl and depression days in Oklahoma, but no effort has been made to present a comprehensive history of the New Deal. Instead, we offer glimpses of various groups and agencies, some public, some private, some state, and federal—all coping with adversity, and trying to forge a rebirth of civilization and the good life in a cauldron of disaster.

All of the essays herein are profusely illustrated, and the volume also includes a photographic collection which is designed to bring the Oklahoma of the thirties into realistic focus. We hope that the essays and the photographs combined will accomplish more than merely trigger harsh memories. We hope they will foster pride in the fact that, whatever the odds, Oklahoma faced and overcame one of the greatest social calamities of modern times and emerged tempered and strong to face an uncertain yet productive future.

I wish to express my thanks and gratitude to the Hardin Foundation of Wichita County which financed the portions of the book written by Professor Monahan and myself, as well as the procurement of many of the photographs. Without their assistance the volume could not have been written. Thanks also to the Faculty Research Committee of

Midwestern State University and similar committees at the institutions of the other authors who provided additional subsidies.

I am grateful to the staff of Moffett Library of Midwestern State University, especially the Director, Melba Harvill, and Interlibrary Loan Director Georgette Gerlach for their able assistance and encouragement. Finally, a special thank you to my secretaries Fran Ethridge and Dianna Roberts, who typed and assisted with the editing of the book in their usual able and dedicated manner.

Kenneth E. Hendrickson, Jr.
Wichita Falls, Texas
February, 1983

Hard Times in Oklahoma

Depression Politics:
Personality and the Problem of Relief

By Danney Goble and James Ralph Scales

The Great Depression means many things in Oklahoma.[1] It meant a young novelist named John Steinbeck locating a place named Sallisaw on the map and creating a fictional family named Joad. It meant a young man from Okemah, Woodie Guthrie—Woodrow Wilson Guthrie, his fiercely anti-Socialist father had named him—blown with the dust, first to California, then to New York, losing his father's political preferences along the way. It meant oil prices plummeting to twenty cents a barrel, the closing of coal mines in the southeastern counties and of lead and zinc mines along the Kansas-Missouri border. It meant food riots in Oklahoma City and anxious national guardsmen patrolling the state. It meant droughts so devastating that hundreds of thousands left the state, the least favored to be named Okies, giving the nation its enduring symbol of human misery, and the migrants an indelible badge of shame.[2]

Politically, the depression brought an era of unprecedented activity and change. The economic disorder altered political fortunes no less than personal fortunes. It ravaged state finance even while the spreading destitution pressed new demands upon desperate state authorities. At the same time, the launching of Franklin Roosevelt's New Deal in 1933 touched off a revolution in federal-state relations and partisan realignments, as well. For all these reasons, the Great Depression became a watershed in state politics.

The election campaign that opened the decade foreshadowed much of the politics to come. Oklahoma's GOP had won stunning victories in the 1920s, when the Republicans elected two United States senators, twice carried the state's electoral college vote, and sent record numbers to the statehouse. In 1930 and long thereafter, the party was reduced to near total impotence, the curse of its identification with economic disaster.

To the Democrats fell the electoral advantage of the depression, but their own party was no less affected by it. The demise of strong Republican opposition ended any semblance of cohesion within the dominant party. The filing period testified to the sudden free-for-all that was Democratic party politics. No fewer than 103 candidates entered as Democrats for fifteen elective state offices, along with record fields for congressional seats and state legislative and judicial posts. Nine candidates sought the gubernatorial nomination in 1930, and the average number of Democratic aspirants for the governorship in the three depression-era elections (1930, 1934, and 1938) would be eleven, roughly twice the average number in the Democratic primaries between 1907 and 1926. The depression's political effect upon the majority party was already evident; the politics of personality had arrived.

The 1930 primary campaign underscored the rise of personal style and the absence of issues. Although every candidate sought to woo the discontented electorate with generous promises and extravagant oratory, the race quickly became a two-man affair.[3] On the one side was Frank Buttram, a millionaire Oklahoma City oilman seeking his first elective office. His inexperience and presumed political innocence were major elements in his appeal. They were complemented by his genial conservatism, generous philanthropy, and unimpeachable integrity.

Buttram's major rival was his opposite in all but the last attribute. William H. "Alfalfa Bill" Murray was a political anachronism, a modern-day version of frontier democracy. Despite his leadership at the time of statehood, he had not won an election since 1914. He had spent most of the preceding decade vainly attempting to colonize the wild frontiers of Bolivia. Only in August, 1929, had he returned, virtually penniless, to Oklahoma, just in time to sense the possibilities of another revolt against the scheming "interests." Borrowing forty-two dollars from the First National Bank of Tishomingo, Murray announced for governor. He wore his familiar white cotton suit, its legs rising above the ankles to reveal six inches of long underwear. Over the summer, he crossed the backroads of the state, subsisting on a diet of cheese and crackers, professing to be certain of victory. "The country folk is aroused," he confidently noted.[4]

Alfalfa Bill was right. The country folk were aroused, and he played to their resentment deliberately and brilliantly. His campaign became a legend of Sooner politics, less for its issues than the candidate's sheer audacity and genius for self-dramatization. While the alarmed metropolitan press raised the banner of dignity and reviled him for his crudities,[5] Murray assumed the role of the courthouse Socrates. He battled the rich, whom he blamed for the depression, scorned the respectable, and, sitting on the hot curbstone of a hundred towns, munched his cheese and crackers. In manner more than cause, the poor had found their champion.

Murray's triumph over the dignified Buttram was the stunning news of the first primary.[6] His margin was swollen by the rising resentment of great wealth which made the state's first runoff a runaway affair. In November, he crushed Ira Hill, the Republicans' gubernatorial sacrifice, by an unprecedented count, 301,921 to 208,575.[7] His inauguration, attended by 12,000 of his faithful followers,

"Alfalfa" Bill Murray. (Courtesy Western History Collections, University of Oklahoma Library)

was Murray's own show. Repeating the prescribed oath of office, administered by his ninety-one year-old father,

Alfalfa Bill asserted his fitness to meet the crisis, firm in the conviction that "running a government is very much like running a farm." With a note of vindictiveness toward his still vocal critics, Murray pledged that "I shall honestly and honorably represent those who choose to call themselves the 'better element,' but this is one time when Oklahoma Indians, niggers, and po' white folks are going to have a fair-minded governor too."[8] From the moment of his swearing-in ceremony, Oklahomans knew that they had a governor of immense personal appeal, a powerful advocate and a dangerous foe.

They also had an executive who became the magnet of state politics in the early depression era. During the four years of his administration, and at sporadic intervals during the remainder of the decade, "Murrayism" was the single, overriding question in Oklahoma politics. To its foes—a sizable legislative bloc, most of the lesser state officers, and nearly all the metropolitan press—Murrayism meant a frightful concentration of power in the hands of an outrageous demagogue.[9] To the governor's ill-coordinated legions, it meant their champion's battle against entrenched wealth, arrogance, and greed.

Few matters so clearly measure Murray's impact as his leadership in the paramount crisis: relief for Oklahoma's stricken people. The total reach of the depression quickly overwhelmed the primitive structure of relief in the state. Except for Confederate veterans' pensions, the state left relief a responsibility of local authorities as late as 1930. Barely adequate in the best of times, county aid was always poorly funded and grudgingly given. In the crisis of mass need, private charity could not begin to bridge the gap. Even including private donations, only $4,500 was recorded for relief efforts in all of populous Pittsburg County as late as 1933. Seventy percent of the total went to the county poor farm. There was nothing at all available for the able-bodied unemployed.[10]

Under Murray's prodding, the 1931 legislature appropriated $300,000 for immediate direct relief. It was far from enough, yet Oklahoma was one of only four states that gave any direct relief at all at the time.[11] The legislative help was quickly exhausted. Murray thereupon exacted "voluntary" contributions of 1.5 percent of the salaries of state employees to replenish the relief fund. He also ordered the highway department to use gasoline tax collections in excess of $1 million to hire the unemployed for public work. Eventually spending $1.2 million for state relief during his administration (plus another $6,000 of his own money), the concerned governor sponsored projects that ranged from the distribution of one million free textbooks for the children of the needy to allowing ten unemployed men to plant vegetable gardens on the unused land between the governor's mansion and the state capitol.[12]

More dramatic was Murray's resort to martial authority. The governor never hesitated to summon the militia to secure what he believed to be justice for the oppressed. Tax sales of farms and homes were halted by his declarations of martial law in eleven counties and the threat of it in others.[13] His orders released poor men arrested as vagrants. After Oklahoma City health officials forbade the practice of feeding hundreds of unemployed men from the surplus of Saint Anthony Hospital's kitchens, the governor retaliated with the threat to declare a military zone around the hospital, ending the city's authority. The same health officers condemned as unsanitary the distribution of substandard skimmed milk sold to the poor by the O. K. Milk Commission, a cooperative of 2,000 farmers in the Oklahoma City area. When M. C. Graham, the association's president, was arrested on complaint of the city health officer, Murray responded in an unusual executive proclamation that granted Graham a full pardon and prevented his future arrest by declaring a military zone of Graham's home, office, and automobile.[14]

After such incidents, no one was disposed to disbelieve the governor when he rang for the adjutant general, and the threat of martial law was usually sufficient to gain his desired objective. One incident humiliated the state's largest enterprise. The Phillips Petroleum Company, which had been supplying commercially worthless free gas from its open pipelines for a year, decided on a very cold day to shut off the supply of its uninvited consumers. Murray gave the company thirty minutes to turn the gas back on. It did.[15]

Such singular incidents, like the primitive state relief projects, could hardly slow the tide of disaster. The plain fact was that the state could not afford to maintain even its routine services, much less assume expensive new relief burdens. Property tax collections had dropped $30 million by 1933, and revenue from the gross production levies skidded downward with petroleum prices. The wonder is not that the state did no more, but that it could do anything at all.

Murray's critics almost immediately charged that his handling of federal funds was riddled with corruption and political favoritism. In response, Washington dispatched Aubrey Williams, FERA liaison officer, to Oklahoma City for a conference with the governor. Perhaps deliberately, Alfalfa Bill was on his worst behavior. Wearing dirty socks and no shoes, the governor met Williams and offered his guest a cup of tea strained through a filthy handkerchief. When he compounded those insults by cursing Roosevelt, Williams stalked out, reporting to the administration that he had found "thieving and favoritism on all sides. I found that every Tom, Dick and Harry in the state was getting relief whether they were unemployed or not." Patience exhausted, national authorities took the administration of relief from the governor's hands in 1934, giving Oklahoma the dubious honor of joining Huey Long's Louisiana with a federalized relief program.[20]

The governor's feud with the New Deal administrators was typical of his approach to both politics and relief. Both were intensely personal, but their effects reached beyond the governor. At the same time, Murray's obstinacy greatly diminished his standing with the Sooner electorate. When he characteristically and presumptuously anointed a slate for state offices in 1934, his popular standing was near its ebb. Virtually every candidate for state office in that year

E. W. Marland. (Courtesy Western History Collections, University of Oklahoma Library.)

hurried to denounce Murray. Murray's designated successor, Tom Anglin of Holdenville, bore the brunt of their attack. Through most of the summer's campaigning, the issue remained, as it had been for four years, Murrayism.

Among the Democrats' gubernatorial aspirants, only one candidate was able to escape the pervasive shadow of Murray. E. W. Marland was that candidate. Ponca City's legendary oilman had entered politics only in 1932, and his service had been as a congressman in Washington, where he had given loyal support to the New Deal. Free from the rancorous old state controversies that divided the remainder of the field, Marland turned his campaign to other matters. "Bring the New Deal to Oklahoma" was his pledge. With those six, simple words, the Marland candidacy offered to transcend the politics of personality.

The Marland effort ignited in the final days before the June primary. Political prophets had expected a runoff between Anglin and J. Berry King with Murrayism as the central issue. In fact, it was Marland who buried the large field, polling 156,885 votes, some 55,000 more than Alfalfa Bill's designated heir, who was the runner-up. With the air of one eager to avoid the recent unpleasantness, Anglin chose not to contest Marland's obvious popularity and generously withdrew from the runoff. While most Sooner Democrats happily lined up behind the victor, Governor Murray played his last spiteful card. For the first time in nearly four decades of public life, Murray broke party lines to endorse the Republican gubernatorial nominee, former senator William B. Pine, against the New Deal's most notable Oklahoma advocate.[21] That defiant gesture was without effect. Marland bested Murray's own performance of four years earlier to establish a new record margin, 365,992 to 243,841.[22]

Few public personalities provide such contrast as Oklahoma's ninth and tenth governors. The one was the self-educated son of a poor Texas farmer, the other a privately schooled patrician.[23] While one was taking his training in the rough school of frontier politics, the other was drawing upon his legal and geological expertise to build the fabled Marland Oil Company, an $85 million empire that stretched across most of the United States and part of Mexico. Against Murray's squalid eccentricities, Marland offered a dramatic contrast. He had lived in self-made grandeur, proudly sharing it as a lordly philanthropist, until his empire collapsed in 1930, when what Marland called the "wolves of Wall Street" unceremoniously deposed the founder and repainted the "Marland" signs to "Conoco." He had turned his humanitarianism—and his rage—to politics. The normally rockribbed Republican voters of the Eighth District sent him to Congress in 1932. The state electorate sent him to Oklahoma City two years later to reverse Murray's obstructionism. He would bring the New Deal to Oklahoma.

In a brief preinaugural address, Marland outlined the meaning of that promise:[24]

> We are coming to a new thought. It is the duty of government to provide every man able to work and willing to work with employment and to take care of those unable to work. . . . Every man in this state who wants to work can be put to work and we can take care of the poor who cannot work. We can give everyone a decent living and a good home in which to rear a family.

Marland wasted no time in indicating the steps necessary to realize that vision. His first message to the 1934 legislature laid out the elements of the "little New Deal" that he would effect in Oklahoma.[25] With 35,000 needy citizens about to be cut from the contracting federal relief rolls, he implored the legislators to appropriate $5 million for immediate state assistance. He also insisted that the money be distributed by the existing, professional, federal relief officials. If relief was the imperative in crisis, Marland felt that state planning was needed for the long road to recovery. He proposed the creation of five new, professionally staffed agencies to coordinate the war on depression and to guide future orderly growth. A planning board would survey the state's resources and oversee their efficient use and conservation. A housing board would build 115,000 subsistence homesteads for the state's needy. A flood control board, modeled on the Tennessee Valley Authority, would supervise the reclamation of depleted soil and build a network of dams for irrigation, power, and recreation. A new industries board would establish state-owned factories to process native products and supply the indigent with necessities. A highway board would disburse state and federal funds and inaugurate a vast public works program and restore one-third of the state's wage earners to productivity.

The price of Marland's proposals was breathtakingly expensive by 1935 budget standards. The five proposed boards would require initial appropriations totaling $7.5 million. When that sum was added to his other requests, Marland was proposing a total state outlay of $35 million. Moreover, that budget would be for a single year, since the governor promised additional recommendations upon the completion of a report by the Brookings Institution on the modernization of Oklahoma government.[26] The fact that the previous legislature had taken the state $4 million deeper into debt while struggling with a *two-year* budget of only $21 million underscored the magnitude of Marland's ambitions.

To help meet these newly assumed obligations, Marland also urged a comprehensive series of new taxes, which featured new levies on the petroleum industry: severance taxes on crude oil, natural gas, and gasoline, along with an increased gross production tax. Oilmen would not be alone in bearing the cost of his vast expansion in state services. The new governor also recommended tripling the one-penny sales tax to finance his relief proposals. A battery of emergency taxes would also tap salaries, insurance premiums, inheritances, cigarette sales, and rental income.

No governor had ever demanded such thoroughgoing changes. None was ever so disappointed. Without new sources of revenue, the administration's visionary plans would come to nothing. The state's business community, from which the necessary tax increases must come, organized the determined resistance to the entire Marland agenda. Within the legislature, that resistance was commanded by the contentious House Speaker Leon C. "Red" Phillips, who was obsessed with economy. Infinitely better suited to legislative infighting than the lordly and naive governor, Phillips and his allies, both within and without the legislature, prepared to scuttle Marland's utopia.

For the first few weeks, Phillips and Marland sparred for power, and the speaker won every skirmish, dismantling the governor's proposals one by one. By the second month of the session, Phillips was able to launch his own counter-offensive. Seeking to balance the budget by minimal appropriations, the Speaker brusquely announced that:[27]

> If the revenue is available for the extra things, we shall adopt such parts as are practicable. . . . The present House of Representatives is progressive enough to care for the needs of the destitute . . . and conservative enough to save the people from the hallucinations of the dreamers.

By the legislature's adjournment, the state's chief dreamer had been awakened to the realities of political power. The proposed five executive boards were trimmed to the most innocuous two. Only a limited flood control board and a powerless planning board won final approval, and their combined annual appropriations were only 12 percent of the figures requested. One-sided compromises had reduced most of the governor's tax proposals by half—no increase over the old rates in most instances. The final state relief appropriation was 75 percent under Marland's request. In fact, it fell short of matching available federal funds from the FERA.[28]

Unable to translate his personal popularity into political power, Marland did as Murray had done. Amid the paralysis at the capitol, two initiative petitions promising relief had appeared independently. The first aimed to relieve the property tax burden by exempting a portion of the value of everyone's dwelling—"homesteads"—from taxation. The second promised more direct relief: old age pensions. The two initiative petitions collected signatures by the thousands, hence the statehouse war moved to a new theater. The embattled governor threw his support behind both proposals, and the legislative leadership submitted rival referenda that offered voters more conservative forms of the same principles. On the homestead exemption issue, the chief difference was that the legislature's version would exclude tax exemptions from existing school levies, which the governor's option would permit. The difference was even greater regarding pensions. The proposal Marland endorsed was considerably more generous, both in the number of persons covered and in the benefits they would enjoy. The governor would make eligible all elderly citizens who had been residents of the state for any five of the previous ten years and lacked "a reasonable subsistence compatible with decency and health." The hastily prepared legislative alternative limited eligibility to the elderly (defined as five years older than Marland's minimum) who had resided continuously in the state for the past fifteen years and received less than $350 annual income. The governor's proposal fixed no constitutional limit on pensions, but the legislative referendum carefully limited maximum pensions to fifteen dollars per person and twenty dollars to any one family. Finally, the legislative proposal provided no constitutional source of funds; the Marland initiative specified financing by heavy levies on gross business income.

It was the governor's pension proposal that drew the greatest fire. The conservative press and his legislative critics assailed the proposal. Associated Industries, lobbyist for the state's chambers of commerce, led the opposition, relying upon delaying tactics. Although the petition contained 180,364 signatures (twice the number necessary for a place on the ballot), desperate businessmen found a valuable ally in Secretary of State Frank C. Carter, the official whose ministerial function included the heretofore routine certification of petitions. Deliberately, Carter dragged out the process by constant delay of hearings on every conceivable technicality. Only seven days before the scheduled special election, Governor Marland, ignoring the endless hearings, asserted gubernatorial prerogative to order the question placed on the ballot.[29]

In the direct test between Marland and the legislative leadership, the governor emerged an easy victor. Voters rejected the legislative form of homestead exemption in favor of a two-to-one approval of the governor's more generous option. Similarly, they overwhelmingly turned down the legislature's idea of old age pensions in favor of the Marland initiative, which passed by the decisive majority of 204,626 to 78,783.[30] The governor's victory proved to be short-lived, however. Responding to a suit filed by Associated Industries, the state supreme court voided the pensions election, holding that Marland had exceeded his constitutional authority in bypassing the obstructionist secretary of state.[31]

A year later, pensions became a reality in Oklahoma, but the credit was not Marland's. The national Social Security Act of 1935 held out the lure of federal matching grants for benefit payments to the aged, the blind, and needy dependent children. States qualified for participation by establishing their own central agencies to administer the system. Establishing its state department of welfare by constitutional amendment in 1936, Oklahoma merely accepted the minimal demands of that federal law. Where the state could exercise discretion (in setting benefit levels and authorizing its share of the financing), it revealed the limits of its new commitment. Oklahoma allowed pensioners a maximum of thirty dollars a month including all other sources of income. The maximum was absolute; it could not be increased even if the federal contribution should exceed thirty dollars. Financing was linked to the regressive sales tax, which was doubled to two cents and earmarked for the new welfare department.[32]

The new relief machinery won voter approval at the 1936 primary elections. Two other elections were notable in that year. President Roosevelt nearly duplicated his landslide victory of four years earlier by beating Republican nominee Alf Landon by more than two to one. Landon carried one county in seventy-seven: Major. If Sooners' affection for the president had not diminished, their support for the governor had. In mid-term, Marland announced for the Senate seat held by anti-New Dealer Thomas Pryor Gore. Although he tried again to exploit New Deal loyalties, Marland's awkward record of failure to establish a state version of it left him a distant second in the four-man first primary. He was outclassed by Fifth District Congressman Josh Lee in the runoff, where Marland took only 38 percent of the vote. Between that election and his record performance two years earlier, the governor's vote total had dropped by nearly 180,000 ballots.[33]

For the remainder of his term, Governor Marland was a spent force. Although he had the satisfaction of seeing his old foe, "Red" Phillips, replaced as Speaker of the Sixteenth Legislature, even that single victory was Pyrrhic. The lawmakers who repudiated Phillips's leadership rejected that of Marland just as decisively. Political power in the legislature fell to the independent committee chairmen. The governor was reduced to the status of the chief clerk, his advice to the assembly politely and routinely ignored. In the end, the lawmakers' work would embarrass the governor even more than the stubborn obstruction of the previous assembly, for this legislature would be forever known as the "Spending Sixteenth."

Understandably, relief was a major source of that reputation. Much of the extravagance was honorable: the nourishment of human life. Despite the recently expanded efforts in Washington and the creation of a state welfare department, thousands of Oklahomans still knew a precarious existence in 1937. Accordingly, the Sixteenth Legislature appropriated a record $7.6 million for direct relief, nearly five times the appropriation of 1935, when the need had been even more acute. But the humanitarian impulse could not be used to rationalize other excesses. Record allotments were made for highways and other public works.

Oklahoma Relief Workers, (Courtesy Western History Collections, University of Oklahoma Library.)

The "Spending Sixteenth" fully earned its nickname by authorizing expenditures of nearly $64 million. That sum was not only triple the state budget when Marland took office, it was also nearly $40 million greater than anticipated tax collections for the coming two years.[34]

The legislature's good deeds had not been entirely altruistic. The lawmakers' generosity of 1937 bypassed the new state welfare department. Legislators insisted that the relief money, much of it matched by federal funds, be distributed by their allies on patronage-ridden and notoriously inefficient county welfare boards. Within a year, the use of welfare funds, including the federal contribution, became a national scandal. Federal investigators discovered that 20,766 of the 69,222 citizens receiving pensions as needy old people were ineligible, many because they were not needy, others because they were not old. In most counties, administration was shaped by local political chieftains, who were never anxious to turn down a worthy voter or loyal party worker. In three counties, the practice of padding the rolls became so notorious that the number of "needy" old people actually exceeded the county's total elderly population. As the federal inquiry proceeded, some legislators pretended great indignation at the "intervention" of the "sorority sob sisters," a derisive reference to professionally trained social workers. In the new adjustments required by the welfare state, there would be recurring rage on the part of elective officials at the prospect that more jobs would go to university graduates, replacing loyal partisans. All passion spent, the solons of 1937 eventually bowed to federal accounting and personnel standards. Their surrender came only after the temporary suspension of federal relief funds to Oklahoma by an appalled Social Security Administration.[35]

Even before the federal relief scandal, Marland's reputation was in shambles. While his own role in the legislative extravagance had been minimal, the governor could hardly plead lack of leadership as a defense; and most observers were quick to blame the failures upon Marland himself. For all the advantages of his background and the breadth of his vision, E. W. Marland was seriously miscast as a political leader. His reputation as a humanitarian was narrowly founded. Private generosity could be extended according to his own means and rules. Publicly funded relief was more than philanthropic good works. Incredibly naive, he had been quite unprepared for the bruising give-and-take of statehouse politics. As governor, he had tried to run the state as though it were his corporation, under a benevolent and farsighted executive who dispatched general commands, the specifics to be worked out by faithful employees who dared not question his wisdom. Only after his ruin could he come to realize that independent department officials and headstrong legislators were very much inclined to dispute his judgements and sabotage his designs, for they owed him neither their jobs nor their salaries. Legislators refused to limit their traditional prerogatives to the modern cause of efficient and impersonal administration. Local leaders declined to relinquish their powers to appointed experts in Washington or Oklahoma City. At bottom, most Oklahomans were unprepared for the swift transition of an agrarian, patronage-minded commonwealth to a social welfare state that supported vast new agencies and required a high degree of administrative skills.

Most of all, the failure of the Marland dream testified to the new realities of Sooner politics in the depression. Despite its recent impressive triumphs—perhaps, indeed, because of them—the Oklahoma Democratic party of the 1930s exactly fit V. O. Key's classic definition of affairs in the one-party South. By the mid 1930s, the party was actually "a holding-company for congeries of transient squabbling factions . . . which fail by far to meet the standards of permanence, cohesiveness, and responsibility that characterize the [ideal of a] political party."[36]

For Marland to have succeeded in bringing the New Deal to Oklahoma demanded that he do what Franklin Roosevelt was doing on a larger scale: assert his leadership over a broad-based but disciplined coalition of voting blocs committed to the pursuit of liberal goals. Oklahoma lacked a governor able to do that. But Oklahoma lacked much more, and even had Marland possessed Roosevelt's political gifts and instincts, he would have failed. Like most states that vainly attempted their own "little New Deals" in the depression, Oklahoma lacked the constitutional and statutory structures flexible enough for change. The state also lacked a tradition of disciplined voter blocs, at least since the demise of the Farmer-Labor Reconstruction League in the early 1920s. No urban political machines, no politically assertive ethnic communities, no rising labor unions stood ready to train their followers in the systematic use of their ballots. At the polls, it was the politics of personality that prevailed, as Sooners cast their ballots on the basis of temporary emotions and fleeting preferences. Though men as widely opposed as Murray and Marland could win elections, neither could call upon a constituency that was either permanent or cohesive. Neither had been able to force party responsibility upon fellow Democrats.

For all their differences, the Murray and Marland governorships suffered a common tragedy. Neither understood the overwhelming economic changes that were testing the rigid political patterns of the state. The one had been unable to evade the impact of the New Deal. The other had been unable to expand it.

Ira Finley. (Courtesy Patrick McGinnis.)

"Share the Work":

Ira M. Finley and the Veterans of Industry of America

By Patrick McGinnis

In Oklahoma, the Great Depression did not cripple a strident boom, for the prosperity proclaimed by Coolidge had never taken root. Following the collapse in farm prices after World War I, the economy of the Sooner state never approached genuine levels of recovery, and matters grew worse as several discoveries of enormous petroleum reserves drove the price of oil steadily downward. Spotty business and agricultural prosperity in a few sections, chiefly the wheat-growing northwest and some urban areas, did almost nothing to alter the general picture of economic decline. Farm tenancy had already begun to spread by the middle twenties, and grew steadily into the thirties. Exacerbating the problem was a series of searing droughts, with those of 1930 and 1934 particularly destructive. Whether on farms or in cities, unemployment, poverty, and despair prevailed in Oklahoma.[1]

Politics appeared to offer little chance of relief. In 1930 the voters chose William H. Murray governor, perhaps in part, at least, because he promised a relief program. Murray spoke for the rural poor and the unemployed, but did not enjoy the support of the more affluent classes, particularly those in Oklahoma City and Tulsa. The governor reluctantly kept his promise of a relief program, but it was minimally effective. Essentially an economic conservative, Murray dedicated himself to a reduction in state expenditures. In fact, he had little choice since a steadily declining revenue base and limited state borrowing power meant that state outlays for all purposes would necessarily decrease.[2] But within limits, the Murray relief program did function with a genuine humanitarian intent.

One of the governor's associates who became involved in the relief effort was Ira M. Finley, a state legislator from the Capitol Hill district of Oklahoma City. A small but extremely energetic and personable man, he was enormously proud of his heritage, which he celebrated with an endless supply of Irish jokes. He was also a magnetic public speaker and he had used his talent to gain election to the lower house from Beckham County in 1922. A former Socialist, Finley became a Democrat following World War I. He had been a railroad union organizer and an official in the United Brotherhood of Maintenance of Way employees, an affiliate of the American Federation of Labor. He had also attended the organizing convention of the Farmer-Labor Reconstruction League at Shawnee that endorsed John C. Walton ("Our Jack") for governor in March of 1922.

Finley became disenchanted with "Our Jack" even before Walton's election to the governorship. In a speech to the Reconstruction League Walton announced that he had not read the League's platform and did not need to read it. "If you're for it, I'm for it," he declared.[3] To Finley, such a statement was the mark of an opportunistic demagogue. When impeachment proceedings were instituted against Walton, Finley voted to impeach the governor on several of the charges made against him. This took courage since Finley in June of 1923 was elected President of the State Federation of Labor, which had been instrumental in the creation of the Farmer-Labor Reconstruction League. Among the Federation's powerful leaders were Luther Langston, like Finley a former Socialist, and Victor Purdy, both staunch Walton men. It was Finley's conviction that he had been chosen president of the labor federation through the machinations of these men, whom he would always thereafter call "labor racketeers." Apparently Langston, Purdy, and their adherents expected Finley to serve largely as a ceremonial executive, while they in fact ran the organization as a personal fiefdom and mainstay of the Walton machine. If so, they had severely misjudged their man. Finley took his duties seriously and actively promoted union recruitment and organization in the state, much of which did not please the monied allies of Walton. As a result, the "racketeers" secured Finley's defeat by Joseph Campbell in 1925 and in 1926 he left the legislature as well.

Soon after the election Finley moved to Oklahoma City and concentrated on private business. In 1930 he ran for the legislature again, and was chosen to represent the Capitol Hill district. Before then he had no particular acquaintance with William H. Murray, although he admired Murray's intelligence and human spirit. At the same time, Finley was puzzled repeatedly by Murray's abrupt rudeness even to those who were genuinely friendly. Said Finley of Murray, "There was a screw loose somewhere."[4]

Despite the quirks of Murray's personality, Finley and the governor established a political alliance that soon became a personal friendship as well. Finley had supported Murray's choice for Speaker of the House and Murray reciprocated by supporting Finley's efforts to have Oklahoma ratify the federal child labor amendment. Probably the association was more personal than political. Murray no doubt saw in Finley a shrewd political talent similar to his own and in addition was probably impressed by his ability to manage disappointed favor-seekers. Whatever the reasons, the two men became very close. For more than two years they went practically everywhere together. When the governor spoke in public Finley would often introduce him, generally poking lighthearted fun at his mentor.

In 1931 Murray asked Finley to serve as director of state relief for Oklahoma. Finley responded that he could not accept such a responsibility and that it might be wiser to have a nonpolitician in the post. He suggested that the former President of Central Normal College in Edmond, Dr. Charles Evans, would be a good choice, and Murray appointed Evans with the understanding that the educator would seek advice from Finley. Finley also agreed to manage the Oklahoma County relief program.

In 1933 the New Deal made significant federal sums available for relief for the first time through the Reconstruction Finance Corporation. Oklahoma was not to benefit extensively, however, since the state's treasury could not provide the necessary matching funds. Moreover, a sharp confict erupted between Murray and the Roosevelt relief agencies over administration. Critics, including many Oklahoma New Dealers, insisted that the Murray administration methods were altogether political; that those defined as "eligibles" for relief were generally Murray supporters.[5] The governor's champions, including Ira Finley, insisted that the charges were false and that for the most part funds were being responsibly and effectively handled.[6]

The result was a visit to the state in August 1933, by Harry Hopkins, FDR's chief relief administrator, and his assistant Aubrey Williams. Although they discovered no fraud, they did insist upon a reorganization of the Murray relief program designed to render the operation less political and accomplish a wider distribution of benefits. Williams, in a letter to Hopkins before the latter's arrival, described the situation in Oklahoma as "desperate."[7] Some of Murray's appointees were dismissed as incompetent, but Williams was apparently impressed with Finley's work, and saw to it that he was appointed Transient Relief Superintendent.[8] It was the beginning of a long and friendly association between the two men, despite Finley's growing disenchantment with the early New Deal relief efforts.

In the midst of his work in the Murray relief program, Finley was constantly reminded of the desperate economic plight of Oklahoma depression victims. Since his Socialist days, Finley had pondered the need, as he saw it, for a single "great labor organization" that could effectively politicize the poor and disadvantaged. In his contacts with state relief personnel, Finley often pursued the possibility of an organization of the unemployed that would agitate for state and federal legislation designed to alleviate unemployment and accomplish a more equitable distribution of wealth. At a conference of county relief directors in the late summer of 1932, Finley and several others developed the idea further; with Finley taking the lead, they incorporated the Veterans of Industry on September 28, 1932. From the beginning the organization was called Veterans of Industry *of America.* In 1937 the charter was amended to reflect the change.

Announcing the organization's first meeting for October 23, Finley identified the group's primary goal as a "share-the-work" approach to be accomplished by a state law that would tax those who worked their employees more than thirty hours a week. The *Oklahoma City Times* identified Finley as Murray's "mouthpiece in some instances."[9] Among others who participated in the incorporation of the VIA were T. B. Williams, C. H. Rogers, and E. D. Billingsley of Oklahoma City; L. C. Watson of Shawnee; W. B. Duffield of Enid; and C. W. McDaniel of El Reno. All had been active in one capacity or another in the Murray relief program.

From the beginning, Finley was the primary initiator of VIA organization drives and the chief spokesman of the group. Elected president at its first meeting, he served in that office for the entire fifteen years of the organization's existence. He gave it its structural scheme and was instrumental in its accomplishments. Undoubtedly much of the Finley influence stemmed from the fact that he put his own money behind the movement. Finley had become relatively prosperous as a salesman of road machinery during the late twenties, and by 1930 was netting nearly $1,300 a month. He was also active in real estate and in early 1931 he rented a second floor from the Gill Feed and Seed Company at 312 1/2 West California Street in Oklahoma City. Two offices faced north overlooking California and restrooms were at the rear. Between ran a large open area which became the VIA meeting hall. It was here that the state headquarters of the organization would be located throughout most of its active life. Rental costs and a large portion of the daily expenses of the organization came directly from Finley's own pocket.[10]

The formation of chapters throughout the state began at once and spread rapidly. A majority of the chapters were to be located in the central, southeastern, southwestern, and northeastern parts of the state, although active and important chapters were to be found in time as far west as Woodward and Enid. This fact reflected the VIA's composition of unemployed or semi-employed oil field workers, railroad laborers, farmers, displaced tenants, and small businessmen. The larger agricultural units of the northwestern part of the state did not produce the type of people to whom the VIA and its program directly appealed. Also, despite a constant public stance as a "non-partisan" organization, the VIA drew closer to the Democratic party than its opponents, and the northwestern counties were traditional Republican strongholds in the state.

Each local chapter of the VIA was under the direction of an executive board of seven chosen by the membership. Officers were selected by the board from among the seven and were empowered to act for the membership unless specifically overruled. Above the local chapters were the congressional district organizations, again directed by an executive board headquartered in Oklahoma City. Finley intended to provide effective leadership at all organizational levels and at the same time give each chapter a large measure of local autonomy. The use of executive boards, however, would enable each level of the organization to take action without endless wrangling over procedural matters and local issues.

The organization grew rapidly, and by October, 1933, Finley claimed 60,000 members. Unfortunately, there is no way these or later figures can be authenticated. While it is entirely possible that Finley's own unabashed enthusiasm may have resulted in a certain exaggeration, it seems reasonable that several tens of thousands of unemployed Oklahomans did give the organization their support at different times and with varying degrees of commitment. In the beginning, and for much of the organization's existence, there were no dues, and the only badge of membership was a small blue card, which bore the VIA slogan, composed by Finley:[11]

> Poverty must be wiped out. No nation can call itself Christian or civilized that permits babes, little children and the aged to suffer for food, clothes and shelter.

Although possession of the card technically entitled the bearer to claim membership in the VIA, it did not, of course, insure his fidelity to the organization or his enthusiasm for its goals. Nevertheless, the cards were distributed by the thousands and proved to be an effective organizational technique.

In November, 1933, the organization produced the first issue of its newspaper, the *V.I.A. Voice*, soon changed to *Labor's Voice.* The sheet was to prove invaluable in maintaining contact between the leadership and the rank and file, and as a recruiting device. The expense of publishing the newspaper quickly became the major item in the VIA budget, a cost that would never be more than partially offset by advertising.

Finley's closeness to Murray and his role as Transient Relief Superintendent contributed to a widespread conviction that the VIA was a front for the governor. The metropolitan press, particularly the Gaylord newspapers in Oklahoma City, held strongly to this idea, despite persistent denials by both Finley and Murray. The opinion was shared by at least some of Murray's political foes and even by a few of his supporters, and it was this fact that indirectly brought an end to Finley's participation in the state relief program. In December, 1933, Aubrey Williams sent William J. Plunkert, who had overseen relief in Alabama, to assess the

Oklahoma program. He was not pleased with what he saw. In a confidential report to Hopkins he characterized Finley as having "limited ability and no imagination."[12] He was particularly disturbed to learn of Finley's presidency of the VIA, which he assumed to be a Murray organization. He attached several copies of the *VIA Voice* to his report and called his superior's attention to articles in the newspaper critical of some of Murray's political opponents. In a tour of the state with Finley, Plunkert found much to criticize, particularly what he conceived to be the total domination of the relief program by Murray henchmen. Returning to Oklahoma City, he informed Murray that the program would have to be changed to be brought under the direction of trained professional social workers, and he demanded Finley's resignation. As Plunkert put it, "The governor was excited and unpleasant and explained in no uncertain terms what he thought, both of the worker and National Administration."[13] Finley was more to the point: "Murray cussed him [Plunkert] out."[14] But Finley did resign.

His dispute with Plunkert was probably inevitable. Finley believed that, as a general rule, professional social workers, or "case workers," as they were more commonly called, were snobbish and condescending and cost far more than they were worth.

With his resignation from the relief program, Finley turned to promoting the VIA full-time. By the end of 1933 the organization's membership was climbing steadily and perhaps exceeded 65,000. More and more of the blue cards were printed and distributed, most of them by chapters in local communities who frequently had to be resupplied by state headquarters. Others were handed out during organizational rallies in various Oklahoma towns and communities. Finley became a tireless traveler, touring the state almost constantly and speaking to gatherings of various sizes. Many rallies were sponsored by local VIA chapters, but Finley and other speakers often would simply stop and begin speaking from street corners, rarely failing to attract interested crowds and often obtaining enough support to begin the organizaton of new chapters.

A unique feature of the VIA was its deliberate inclusion of blacks. This policy reflected Finley's determination that racial discrimination and exploitation of blacks be ended. In 1924 Finley had attracted the political support of Roscoe Dunjee, a prominent leader of the black community of Oklahoma City and publisher and editor of the *Black Dispatch.* At Finley's insistence, blacks received a portion of the relief assistance during the Murray administration, and Finley had placed Dunjee in charge of its distribution in Oklahoma City's "black town." Dunjee became an enthusiastic member of the VIA and attracted a sizable black membership.[15]

By inviting blacks to join the organization, Finley was taking a large chance. Oklahoma was rigidly segregated, and the reign of terror fomented by the Ku Klux Klan in the twenties was a fresh memory. Finley's approach was to attempt to convince white members that continued degradation of blacks would only serve to hold down all members of the laboring class. He did not, however, suggest support for social equality or the organization of integrated chapters. To have done so, he said, would have risked a schism in the VIA. Instead, blacks were organized into separate chapters, a practice that won Dunjee's cooperation. The policy was successful both in attracting a large black membership and in ameliorating any tendency of white members to object to it. Finley said there was no racial trouble in the VIA and he gave Dunjee the credit for this success.

New Deal relief programs continued to prove inadequate to meet the needs of indigent Oklahomans, and the VIA called for more effective measures. The Federal Emergency Relief Administration, established during the hundred days of 1933, was totally removed from Murray's control. It came in for special criticism by the Veterans of Industry. Professing disinterest in whether the agency was controlled by state or federal authority, Finley criticized "the very nature of the thing." The VIA, he insisted, was interested in "seeing jobs provided for the workers. Jobs that will pay more than a living wage [sic]. Jobs that will enable the workers to produce new wealth and to consume such products [sic]."[16]

The brief experiment in work relief conducted by the Civil Works Administration in the fall and winter of 1933-34 impressed the VIA leadership as greatly preferable to a dole, but it too was decried as insufficient. In assessing the problem of unemployment, some of the old socialist rhetoric and ideology emerged from Finley's past. Insisting that the CWA was little better than a dole, he wrote: "We must not forget the fact that there is just as much wealth in this country as ever and that the workers are ready to produce many times the wealth we now have if they can only have the use of the machine. . . ."[17] Finley emphasized the theme of "production for use" and insisted upon government action to provide jobs for the unemployed.

Throughout the thirties, the most actively promoted of the VIA programs was an old-age pension. The idea of state-financed retirement was not original with the VIA, of course, but no other organization in Oklahoma, with the possible exception of the Townsend Clubs, was as outspoken in its support of the concept. As early as 1933, petition campaigns were underway to obtain a pension that would provide a living income for those beyond their productive years. On April 15, 1934, the state executive board met in Oklahoma City and heard a report from VIA secretary Lorena Keeler that 170,000 names had been secured on petitions asking President Roosevelt to propose a federal pension plan giving every citizen over age fifty a pension of $50 a month. Keeler demonstrated her enthusiasm for the idea by volunteering to take the petitions to Washington herself, and before the week was out she had left Oklahoma City by car, accompanied by her daughter. A selfless gesture, her trip made little impression in the capital. As she reported in *Labor's Voice* on May 18, she interviewed nearly seventy people, and although some expressed cautious interest, they gave her little encouragement. She was particularly disgusted with the reaction of the Oklahoma delegation, which she found either complacent or patronizing. In time the VIA would attract the support of some Oklahoma congressmen, but following Keeler's return, it apparently decided to concentrate its efforts on securing state action in providing old age pensions.

Pension financing, suggested Finley, could be obtained by a manufacturer's sales tax in the beginning, to be followed by increased income taxes, an inheritance tax, and a gross production tax. In November, 1934, in an editorial he expressed resentment that "the VIA plan has been agitated by a group of people under the Townsley [sic] plan who have entered the field two years after the VIA. . . ."[18]

Whether because of pressure from the Townsendites, the VIA, or other pension advocates, the normally conservative Oklahoma legislature called for a referendum to provide an old age pension. The VIA was naturally suspicious, and Finley editorialized that the proposal should not fix age or benefit limits, but permit the legislature to regulate the program. He and the other members of the state executive board were fearful that a law too narrowly drawn would be deliberately designed to fix benefits at a low level and age requirements. It was an accurate prophecy. The Legislature proposed a constitutional amendment that would have, in Finley's opinion, practically prevented a pension in Oklahoma. Not only did it provide for funding through a general sales tax which would fall most heavily on the poor, it also included a requirement that pension recipients be denied the suffrage. The VIA found these provisions particularly objectionable.

On the night of May 28, 1935, a group representing several organizations met at Farmers Union headquarters in Oklahoma City to plan both an old-age pension petition and a graduated land tax petition. Throughout the thirties, and after, the VIA and the Farmers Union worked closely together and often held joint meetings. The alliance, based on common populist principles and somewhat overlapping membership, centered on the close personal friendship of Ira Finley and Tom Cheek, Oklahoma Farmers Union President, who like Finley, was a former Socialist. Cheek and Finley had been friends since the old days in Elk City and were in close agreement on most political issues. The May 28 gathering appointed Finley to a committee to draft an old-age pension initiative petition. One was quickly drawn up and presented to a large VIA convention at the Oklahoma

City fairgrounds on June 1. Essentially it was the plan already adopted by the VIA leadership except that it called for thirty dollars a month instead of fifty. A note of restraint had entered the rhetoric of *Labor's Voice.* Cautioning against inflation and also conscious of Oklahoma's meager tax base, the editor insisted that "thirty dollars a month was as much as can be expected by a state."[19] Once more he expressed reservations about the Townsend Plan.

Volunteers circulated the petitions enthusiastically during the summer of 1935 and on August 16, they were delivered to the office of Secretary of State Frank Carter. In all, 9,242 petitions bore the names of 180,364 Oklahomans. Governor E. W. Marland stopped by Carter's office to congratulate Finley and his organization. The referendum election was set for September 24.

Almost at once opposition to the proposal crystallized. It came most vocally from the Oklahoma State Chamber of Commerce, which warned its members that adoption of the VIA-Farmers Union plan would cost over $36 million and that its attendant sales tax would seriously injure retail merchants. Most importantly the chamber began a vigorous effort to invalidate a sufficient number of signatures to have the petitions thrown out. Carter made little effort at impartiality, routinely giving the chamber lawyers more than ample time to examine the petitions and file their challenges. The *Daily Oklahoman* and the *Oklahoma City Times* published numerous editorials denouncing the pension proposal. By mid-September, with only a short time remaining before the election, Carter still had not certified the petitions for inclusion on the ballot. To Finley and the other VIA leaders the delay was clearly an effort to defeat the popular will. But on September 17, Marland came to the rescue, or so it appeared. He issued an executive order removing the petitions from Carter's control and certified the pension proposal for inclusion on the ballot.[20] Prior to the election, over 100,000 copies of *Labor's Voice* carefully instructing its readers how to vote were distributed by volunteers. State headquarters ordered that not one copy of the special edition "be allowed to fall on the ground."[21]

The election was a stunning triumph for the VIA, the Farmers Union, and the labor unions that had supported the petition effort. Not only did the pension proposal win, but the voters also enacted a homestead exemption measure supported by the VIA. They defeated question 209, the legislature's pension plan amendment, which Finley had called a "joker." Finley claimed that credit for the victory belonged to his organization and to its friends in the Farmers Union. Marland, in a move clearly designed to gain support from the VIA, appointed a three-man old-age pension commission composed of Finley, Cheek, and state labor Commissioner Pat Murphy, an ally of the VIA.

The commission never formally met. Chamber of Commerce attorneys immediately filed suit to prevent implementation of the new law on the grounds that Marland had had no authority to place the initiated question on the ballot by decree. In February, 1936, the Oklahoma State Supreme Court ruled the pension law invalid.[22] Finley and Cheek concluded that Marland had not acted in good faith—that he had expected all along that the court would not approve his actions, and that he had acted to win political support from the VIA and the Farmers Union and to prepare for a weaker pension plan of his own. Criticism of the governor became increasingly strident in *Labor's Voice* and Finley was convinced that the VIA had been doublecrossed.

A new petition was quickly prepared. Like the first it provided for benefits of approximately thirty dollars a month but raised the age requirement to sixty. Detecting a potentially productive issue, Marland had his supporters draw up yet another proposal. The governor's plan was objectionable, said Finley, because it would provide meager benefits, be unfairly and unsoundly financed, and was designed as a patronage vehicle for the governor. The Marland measure was placed on the ballot for a vote on July 7, 1936, a date which the VIA was unable to meet in its campaign for signatures in support of its own plan. Finley and Cheek strongly opposed the Marland-sponsored measure and urged its defeat.

But the governor's measure won voter approval and by mid-August a nine-member board had been appointed to administer the program. If the governor had, as Finley charged, used pensions as a political ploy, it had done him little good. On the same day his pension plan was approved, Marland was defeated in the Democratic senatorial primary by Josh Lee, who enjoyed informal VIA support. The VIA continued to criticize the new pension law, and the circulation of petitions continued in behalf of the organization's own plan. However, in early October, Secretary of State Frank Carter, citing an insufficient number of valid signatures, dismissed the second VIA pension plan.[23] Despite these setbacks, the organization continued to agitate for what it considered an adequate pension.

Defeat of the VIA pension proposal did not dampen enthusiasm for the organization. A series of adult education classes had been started as early as 1933, and particularly among the black chapters, the response was great. The curriculum of these classes, which were often taught by WPA-employed instructors, was largely confined to basic skills: reading, composition, economics, history, mathematics, typing, and other commercial subjects. Classes were held regularly in the VIA hall and under the auspices of other chapters throughout the state. They were one of the most lasting benefits achieved by the VIA in its approximately fifteen-year existence.[24]

By the time of the old-age pension campaign of 1935, *Labor's Voice* claimed 125,000 members. Since efforts to establish chapters outside Oklahoma were not successful, the organization remained almost exclusively an Oklahoma affair.

To a significant degree, the function of the local chapters was social. VIA chapters provided opportunities for community visits, pie suppers, Christmas parties, and dances. Several chapters organized orchestras or quartets, and numerous amateur composers wrote songs to honor and inspire their comrades. More politically purposeful, perhaps, but still entertaining, were frequent state and congressional district conventions. Delegates traveled to these gatherings however they could, often by filling flat-bed trucks and dilapidated automobiles, or even walking if they did not live too far from the convention sites. The conventions usually debated and enacted resolutions demanding more government action in behalf of the unemployed, reforms in the administration of relief, and enactment of the entire VIA program. State and federal politicians often spoke, but this particular practice became time-consuming and was eventually de-emphasized. Although the state conventions were usually planned and directed by Ira Finley and the other members of the state executive board, they were not dominated by them. On more than one occasion resolutions were presented, and occasionally adopted, with which Finley did not entirely agree.[25]

The VIA's most energetic efforts were directed towards providing jobs for the unemployed. Creation of the Works Progress Administration in 1935 provided the first opportunity for even a semblance of what the VIA had in mind, although certainly WPA jobs were never as plentiful as the Veterans of Industry wished.

In order to take fullest advantage of what was available, the leadership placed heavy emphasis upon the organization of WPA workers. The key to this effort was the function of local grievance committees in those communities where WPA work was going on. How many WPA workers troubled to join the VIA is not documented, but the proportion was probably significant. As the program became established, state VIA headquarters was increasingly swamped with grievance pleas. Many of these it could handle by communicating with state and local WPA superintendents, but Finley insisted that most of them should more properly be taken care of at the local chapter level. The problem was essentially one of educating WPA workers as to the nature of their rights and of instructing local grievance boards in the proper procedures for receiving and filing grievances. The very newness of the works projects approach was seen as an opportunity to help VIA members qualify under some of the skilled work classifications.[26]

Largely because of Finley's efforts state WPA administrators cooperated with the VIA, although some resistance showed itself among local project bosses. On August 20, 1935, Fred Larue, seventh district WPA administrator, and J. S. Maloney, his assistant, appeared at a meeting of a VIA executive committee on the courthouse lawn at Hobart. Larue urged the committees to help county commissioners and city officials work out projects sufficient to employ the 8,500 unemployed workers in his district and Finley emphasized the importance of organizing in each community.[27]

Project bosses often behaved as though their chief responsibility was to work their crews as hard as possible and to interpret their instructions narrowly.[28] Frequently, VIA intervention prevented the violation of worker rights and helped to correct abuses.[29] For example, in late October, complaints were made that foremen and supervisors in Tonkawa had ordered workers either to work in the rain or return in the afternoon to be checked by the timekeeper. The local committee called state headquarters, which in turn complained to the district director of labor management who promised that the practice would not continue.[30] Similar complaints came from other communities. Claiming that the settlement of complaints proved the value of the VIA, *Labor's Voice* insisted that "thousands" of abuses would never occur simply because "those who would be tempted . . . know full well . . . that [because of the VIA] they cannot get away with it."[31] The editor also pointed out that WPA workers who were not members of the VIA nevertheless had the right to appeal to the grievance committees as did members.

Despite frequent involvement by state headquarters, the primary initiative for settlement of WPA worker grievances came from the local chapters. Evidence of strong action by the locals is abundant in *Labor's Voice*. In August, 1936, C. E. Hobaugh, Financial Secretary of El Reno Chapter No. 2, wrote Finley to tell how his group handled the grievance problem. A committee of three VIA members would be appointed on each WPA project to handle problems on the spot. If they were unsuccessful, a county committee was to consider the matter, with a final referral, if necessary, to state headquarters. Finley called the letter a "typical report from wide awake VIA organizations."[32]

By the fall of 1936, the number of WPA projects in Oklahoma was declining. The original appropriation was virtually exhausted and rising criticism of the relief agency had further inhibited its funding. The VIA adamantly protested cutbacks to the Oklahoma congressional delegation. In early October local VIA executive boards were urgently requested to gather statistics on unemployment in their communities for transmittal to Senator Elmer Thomas, an enthusiastic supporter of both the WPA and the VIA. Because of growing conservative opposition to the works program, largely stemming from charges that it had been used to campaign for Roosevelt in 1936, and also because of FDR's own reservations about a permanent relief program, the results were not satisfactory. Determined to do what he could, Ira Finley left Oklahoma City on April 6, 1937, on the first of two trips to Washington, D.C.[33] Meeting with Aubrey Williams, director of the National Youth Administration, whose projects in Oklahoma also had VIA support, Finley was accompanied by Houston Wright, Oklahoma NYA director. Williams was well informed about the VIA, since Finley had kept him on the mailing list of *Labor's Voice* since 1933. Williams expressed sympathy with the VIA program and promised to do what he could to enlarge NYA projects in Oklahoma.[34] On April 13, Finley addressed the Oklahoma congressional delegation at a luncheon in the speaker's dining room in the capitol basement. Emphasizing the severe impact of the protracted drought, Finley insisted that because of Oklahoma's basically agricultural economy, the depression had hurt the Sooner state worse than most others. Citing grim statistics on unemployment, Finley praised the entire VIA program and pleaded with the solons to help enact a truly comprehensive federal works program and, until that could be done, to appeal to the WPA and NYA to "give more consideration" to Oklahoma's plight.[35] It was a heady moment for the former section hand, but a conservative tide was running and all that could be accomplished was a compromise bill that amounted to a severe reduction of public works appropriations, not only for Oklahoma, but for the entire nation. Orders went to state WPA administrators that one of every four WPA workers was to be removed from the rolls.

Refusing to admit failure, and petitioned by his membership, Finley returned to Washington on June 7, and this time he met with Harry Hopkins. Senator Thomas had arranged the interview, and Finley was accompanied by Congressman Sam Massingale and by George McElroy, secretary to Senator Josh Lee.[36] Hopkins heard Finley out but could give him little encouragement. He told the VIA president that although he knew of Oklahoma's need, and sympathized with it, the reduced congressional appropriations left him little choice. Finley was impressed with Hopkins's basic concern for the "forgotten man," but was disappointed by the realities of reduced expenditures. He returned to Oklahoma understandably discouraged but intent upon promoting further the VIA program and, if possible, determined to launch the movement in other states.[37] As long as the WPA lasted, the VIA grievance committees functioned, but the decline in work relief necessarily lessened the organization's impact. In the final analysis, the VIA program, essentially a radical-progressive agenda, was coming up against the conservative reaction that would, by 1939, bring an effective end even to the moderate reforms of the New Deal.

Energetic commitment to the organization's goals, however, continued unabated, and its impact on Oklahoma politics, at least, was to be significant. Despite Finley's contention that the VIA was a "nonpartisan" organization, many of its critics believed it to be essentially a machine for a political opportunist impatiently weighing his chances. There may have been a grain of truth in this contention in the sense that Ira Finley, certainly no modest man, would have undoubtedly taken advantage of any clear opportunity to use his support within the organization to win elective office. But it cannot be maintained that these intentions, if they existed, were fundamentally selfish. Finley was essentially an idealist—philosophically a practical Socialist of the Eugene Debs school. Among his closest friends was Oklahoma Socialist editor Oscar Ameringer, who, although not a member of the VIA, admired its program and its leadership. Certainly no evidence exists that Finley's egotistical idealism ever obscured his practical assessment of Oklahoma politics. The best evidence of this side of Finley's nature was revealed in the Oklahoma gubernatorial primary campaign of 1938. The question was who would succeed E. W. Marland, who could not succeed himself. For the VIA leadership and particularly for Ira Finley, the possibilities were not encouraging. As early as 1935, William H. Murray was rumored to be considering the race. Others who subsequently filed, in addition to Murray, were former governor John Walton, a member of the corporation commission, Colonel William S. Key, until May of 1937 state director of the WPA, and Leon C. Phillips, speaker of the Oklahoma House of Representatives. As Finley and Cheek reflected upon the possibilities, they were distressed at the prospect of Murray, Key, or Walton in the governorship. Finley's personal affection for Murray was tempered by the former governor's extreme opposition to the New Deal. Murray had even shared an Oklahoma City platform with Alfred Landon in 1936. Key, felt Finley, was little better. Although he had resigned as state WPA director to make the race, complaints reached Finley from the VIA membership that WPA workers were being pressured to support the former director. With Murray in the race, Finley feared the vote might be split so as to elect neither Murray nor Key.

Late in 1937 Finley and Cheek visited Murray at his farm near Broken Bow where they found the former governor working in his garden. Finley urged Murray not to enter the governor's race, but to file for a position on the state supreme court. When Murray made it clear that he would nevertheless seek the governorship, Finley replied that he could not support him. Murray dismissed his visitors with scant courtesy. On the drive back to Oklahoma City, Cheek suggested that Finley make the race. He could not win, of course, there was no money for that, but by taking votes from Murray and Key, Finley might be able to throw the race to Phillips.[38]

That is essentially what happened. The poorly financed Finley campaign made Key and Walton its primary targets, identifying them both as the "stooges" of special interests. Murray was characterized as an old friend who had fallen sadly behind the times and who deserved no progressive support. Little mention was made of Phillips, for whom Finley had some respect, largely because of his opposition to the Marland organization during his tenure as Speaker of the House of Representatives. Moreover, at the VIA Convention in Oklahoma City, in January of 1938, Phillips had expressed his support for the VIA and its program.[39]

Despite a visit to the state by President Roosevelt, who came in support of Key, Phillips won the primary election by a plurality of fewer than 3,000 votes over Key, his closest rival. Murray was third with 148,000 votes, Walton fourth with slightly more than 45,000, and Finley was fifth with 37,000.[40] If it may be assumed that had Finley not been in the race his votes would have gone predominantly to Murray, certainly some of them would have been cast for Key,

Sixth Annual Convention, VIA, January 16, 17, 1938 Oklahoma City. (Courtesy Patrick McGinnis.)

giving him the election. In short it may be argued that Phillips owed his election to Finley. Certainly that was Finley's assessment.

The closeness of the VIA and the Oklahoma Farmers Union centered around the personal friendship of Ira Finley and Tom Cheek, and was greatly strengthened by their common support of a graduated land tax. Its stated purpose was to prevent consolidation of land in large holdings and especially to discourage absentee landlordism. Since their Socialist days, Finley and Cheek had supported the general concept, and the spreading of farm tenancy in the twenties and thirties stimulated interest in the proposal among the rural unemployed, many of whom had been dispossessed through foreclosures and tax sales, only to see land they had cultivated taken over by absentee owners. Part of the original VIA program had endorsed "land for those who till it," and the graduated land tax was designed essentially to preserve relatively small, family farm units.[41]

In 1935, along with old-age pension and homestead exemption petitions, the VIA and the Farmers Union initiated a graduated land tax plan. It applied only to farm-

land, specifically exempting timber and grazing land, and it would have provided an additional tax of $50 per thousand of assessed valuation on all land over 640 acres or valued in excess of $12,000 owned by one person or by a corporation. The new taxes were to begin five years after approval of the measure, and both the tax and the provisions of its application could be periodically altered by the legislature.[42] Although only 95,000 valid signatures were required to have the measure placed on the ballot, the VIA and the Farmers Union submitted it in August of 1935 with over 170,000 attached. As in the case of the old-age pension measure, lawyers for the state Chamber of Commerce immediately filed challenges. The result was a protracted legal struggle between the chamber and land tax supporters. After extended delays, the state Supreme Court in November, 1937, appointed a referee to begin *de novo* hearings on the validity of the signatures. Not until February of 1940 did the referee notify the court that enough signatures were valid to have the measure placed on the ballot. Even then, Chamber of Commerce attorneys succeeded in delaying certification of the proposal for several months. It finally appeared on the general election ballot on November 5, 1940.

At first it appeared that the land tax had been adopted. Over 450,000 votes were counted in its favor and only about 170,000 were cast against it. The results were vivid evidcnce of the efforts of the VIA-Farmers Union alliance. But in the final tabulation the tax was defeated by the "silent vote." Over 900,000 persons had voted in the presidential election and state law provided that a majority of that number was necessary to pass an initiated act in a general election. Another 15,000 votes would have enacted the amendment.[43]

Immediately the VIA attempted to have the legislature call a special election on the graduated land tax. Such an election would avoid the "silent vote" obstacle and would apparently have the support of Governor Phillips, who wanted an amendment compelling the state to have an annually balanced budget. The governor's support was perfunctory, however; and in the end the House of Representatives refused by a vote of 55 to 53 to include the land tax in a special election call. The House vote followed a heated debate in which some opponents denounced the graduated land tax as "communistic." Oklahoma City representative Ila Huff, an opponent of the land tax, called for an FBI investigation of Ira Finley, charging that he had coerced WPA workers into paying dues to the VIA.[44] Finley was later cleared of any wrongdoing.

By the summer of 1941, the Veterans of Industry of America was suffering a decline in membership and mounting financial problems. Born in the depression, and comprised mostly of unemployed laborers, the organization could not cope with a slowly but steadily improving economy. By late 1941 defense contracts, an increasing demand for Oklahoma petroleum, rising farm prices, and the draft meant that thousands of VIA members had little time for the conventions, socials, and petition drives that had energized the organization. A falling membership meant falling dues collections, and Finley's own purse could not support the mounting deficit. In July of 1941 the VIA affiliated with the General Welfare Federation of America, an old-age pension group headquartered in Washington, D.C. The next year *Labor's Voice* became the *General Welfare Reporter*, edited by Ira Finley and published in Oklahoma City.[45] Throughout the war years Finley tirelessly wrote and spoke for his remaining members, but the United States had turned conservative. In November, 1946, when the Republicans captured control of Congress, an enlarged national old age pension plan seemed very remote. At about the same time, Finley's wife became seriously ill, reinforcing his discouragement. The few remaining active VIA chapters met in Oklahoma City for the last time in the early spring of 1947, and although several people voiced a desire to begin reorganizing, the movement was practically defunct. The last issue of the *General Welfare Reporter* appeared in March and featured an emotional editorial by Finley announcing that he could not continue as president and editor.[46] He terminated the lease at 312 1/2 West California and several filing cabinets full of VIA records were hauled to the city dump.

The historic significance of the VIA does not lie primarily in the laws it helped to write and enact, even though it could claim partial responsibility for homestead exemption and old age pension laws. Although the latter was not exactly the VIA plan, its passage in 1935 was due largely to the interest stimulated by the organization in its sustained petition drive. It also publicized the workings of the law and assisted many Oklahomans in applying for benefits which it constantly agitated to have increased.

Far more significant was the deliberate effort by the Veterans of Industry to organize WPA workers and to protect their rights through the operation of grievance committees. Probably in no other state were public works laborers as strongly organized and as effectively instructed and represented as in Oklahoma. Unable to prevent constrictions of the works program, the VIA nevertheless secured the cooperation of both federal and state WPA officials in a more equitable distribution of projects and a fairer operation of them.

Almost as important were the adult education classes. Hundreds of Oklahomans learned a variety of skills they would otherwise probaby not have had, and many even became literate thanks to the VIA. A unique feature of the organization, especially visible in the operation of its educational program, was its overt biracial composition. Many Oklahoma blacks secured a modicum of political and social recognition through the VIA that would otherwise have been denied them. Through a carefully cultivated friendship with Roscoe Dunjee and other Oklahoma black leaders, Ira Finley enabled the VIA to repair a small portion of the racial and social disruption of the twenties. Although not strictly integrated at the chapter level, the VIA consistently preserved racial harmony within its ranks, and when contrasted with other Oklahoma organizations in the thirties, particularly labor unions, its record in lowering racial barriers is impressive. Strengthened by a strenuously energetic leadership and sustained by an enthusiastic and politically intelligent membership, the Veterans of Industry of America provided an active protest to the Great Depression in Oklahoma.[47]

Hard Times for Children:
Disease and Sickness During the Great Depression

By D. Clayton Brown

In 1930, when the Great Depression began, Oklahoma was still in the process of becoming a modern state. Her recent entry into the Union in 1907 gave her a comparative disadvantage with other states in the field of social services, a field dependent on tax support and time to organize. Exemplifying these difficulties was the condition of the state's health facilities. Although progress had been made, facilities were generally lacking, with a subsequent effect on the quality of health of the inhabitants.[1] Partly accounting for these circumstances was the poor status of rural health, a problem in many states. Rural residents lacked many of the advantages associated with good health: an adequate supply of physicians, properly equipped hospitals and clinics, and the modern conveniences of home life conducive to hygienic living. More significant, however, was the lack of resources of the state government and to some extent a lack of commitment by the medical profession to improve health.[2]

Indicative of Oklahoma's status in regard to public health was her late entry into the Birth and Death Registration Areas. These Areas were inaugurated to provide the United States Public Health Service (PHS) with a mechanism for collecting from the states the data showing the occurrence of births and deaths. To be included in the Areas, a state had to have the machinery to collect the records of 90 percent of all births and deaths occurring within its borders. The Death Registration Area began in 1880 with two northeastern states and the District of Columbia, while the other Area started in 1915. Oklahoma qualified and joined both in 1928, one of the last states to be included. Statistical data on rural births and deaths were, therefore, reasonably accurate by the thirties, but information listing the cause of death and records pertaining to illness and physical impairments were not wholly reliable in some states.[3]

Causes of death were often described in ambiguous terms, and many physicians used a nomenclature more akin to folklore than medical science. For all age groups, common causes of death were listed as yellow jaundice, dropsy, brain fever, locked bowels, acute indigestion, convulsions, and "summer complaint." Morbidity records were equally confusing because many rural physicians were poorly trained. Many mistakenly diagnosed symptoms as illnesses. Proper training was most lacking in pediatrics, because it was a relatively new medical specialty. On this subject the Oklahoma Bureau of Maternity and Infancy complained that "few physicians, especially those practicing in rural areas, have had opportunity to prepare themselves. . . ."[4] Reporting of illnesses by county registrars, even when diagnoses were correct, was sometimes disorganized and unsystematic.

In 1930 the overwhelming proportion of the Oklahoma population lived in rural areas. The total was 1,574,539 persons, or 65.7 percent. Farm children numbered 584,677, slightly more than 37 percent of the rural inhabitants. For the whole state, one out of four persons, 24.4 percent, was a rural inhabitant under fifteen years of age. Urban children were less numerous, totaling 224,136 or 27.2 percent of the urban population. Altogether there were 808,813 persons fourteen or younger, about one-third of the state's population. The preponderance of rural life was evident in 1930 when only five counties had a majority population living in incorporated areas of 2,500 or more: Oklahoma (Oklahoma City), Garfield, Kay, Tulsa, and Washington. Sixteen cities reported a population over 10,000, but there were twenty-seven counties with no urban inhabitants, meaning these counties had no town numbering above 2,500. The preponderance of rural children, who were less likely to enjoy the benefits of good sanitation and medical care, contributed to the state's rate of childhood diseases, although a clear differential in urban-rural health was not always possible.[5]

Oklahoma's infant mortality rate in the thirties was surprisingly below that of the whole United States. During the

COMPARATIVE INFANT MORTALITY RATE IN OKLAHOMA AND THE UNITED STATES FOR 1930-1939

YEAR	OKLAHOMA	UNITED STATES
1930	60.7	64.6
1931	51.5	61.6
1932	50.0	57.6
1933	56.4	58.1
1934	60.5	60.1
1935	54.6	55.7
1936	60.0	57.1
1937	56.6	54.4
1938	49.0	51.0
1939	49.7	48.0

Source: Bureau of the Census, *Vital Statistics of the United States, 1939, pt.1* (Washington, 1941), p. 23.

years 1930-1933 and 1938 the Sooner State reported a lower rate of deaths under one year of age than the national average. The greatest difference occurred in 1931 when the rates were 51.5 and 61.6 deaths per 1,000 births respectively. For the whole decade Oklahoma's average rate was 54.9 compared with the national average rate of 56.8.

No pronounced differential was apparent in the state's rural and urban infant mortality rates, another surprising feature. In the mid-twenties, the urban rate in the United States fell for the first time below the rural rate owing to the development of sanitation and public health facilities in cities. For the two-year period of 1936-1937, the Oklahoma Public Health Department reported a rate in the state's five urban counties of 60.4 per 1,000 births. For the twenty-seven wholly rural counties the rate was 58.3.[6] Because of the poorer health care in the countryside, the opposite would have been expected. Caution must be exercised when measuring rural infant deaths, however, because all deaths were recorded by place of occurrence and not place of residence. Many farm families took their children into towns and cities in cases of extreme illness, and that natural tendency drove up urban rates. "Increasing proportions of births and infant deaths of rural residents," the PHS noted, "have been occurring in urban hospitals."[7] At the same time there was some question about the "completeness" of registering births and deaths in some states, particularly those where the registration system was new. And the completeness was most questionable in rural reporting; the Census Bureau gauged Oklahoma's completeness of birth reporting at 84 percent in 1940.[8]

Oklahoma's racial differentials in infant deaths conformed with the national pattern. For whites and non-whites in 1937, the state's figures were 52.7 and 94.0 respectively and for the United States they were 50.3 and 83.2. The higher non-white rate in Oklahoma was owing partly to the Indian population of the state. On a county by county basis Oklahoma also had a wide variation in infant deaths. McIntosh County reported a rate of 108.6 for 1936-1937, but its neighboring counties on both sides, Hughes and Haskell, reported 45.4 and 43.5 respectively for the same period. On the other hand, western and eastern counties where geographic conditions contrasted sharply showed no marked difference.[9]

Child deaths originated from a variety of causes and circumstances, many of which were preventable. Superstition among families worsened the difficulty of compiling accurate records; some families attributed the loss of a loved one to the "stretches" or "fits" and "griping in the stomach." But respiratory illnesses—pneumonia, influenza, and tuberculosis—accounted for the largest proportion of deaths for children under fourteen in 1930. Pneumonia, frequently a secondary infection that brought death, struck the most often, killing 935 children that year. Child deaths from pneumonia were proportionately higher than adults because they accounted for 59.7 percent of the total pneumonia deaths, though children comprised 33.7 percent of the state's population. For the whole nation pneumonia deaths in children were 32.6 percent of the total pneumonia deaths, demonstrating that Oklahoma children ran a much greater risk and incidence of the disease. Throughout the thirties pneumonia remained the number one killer in the state, though by 1939 it had reduced its claim to 468 young lives. The large rural population undoubtedly contributed to the high rate since farm housing, particularly during the Great Depression, was substandard and conducive to respiratory infections.[10]

Influenza was another respiratory disease ranking among the worst killers. It was the fourth worst killer in 1930 and 1933 with an age-specific death rate of 23.8 and 31.6 per 100,000 respectively. It climbed to third position in 1937 and 1939 with the rates at 25.3 and 11.4 respectively.

A poorly understood disease, influenza was frightening because of its devastating toll in the swine flu epidemic of 1918-1919. During the thirties, however, Type A and B influenza spread through the United States on several occasions, and Oklahoma certainly had the same strain. In 1939 slight improvements in treatment, plus the absence of a major epidemic, reduced the total deaths for children under fourteen in Oklahoma to ninety-three, but the significance of influenza becomes apparent on a comparative basis. By computing the percentage of total deaths in the state caused by influenza among children under fourteen, Oklahoma ranked fifth in the United States. Through this technique of computation, one finds that Oklahoma had a percentage figure of .0096 compared with .0045 for the whole nation. Sooner children obviously ran a greater risk of death during flu epidemics than most children.[11]

Tuberculosis was the third worst respiratory killer, but it was not regarded as a children's disease since it struck adults with much greater frequency. In 1930 tuberculosis of all forms had an age-specific death rate among children under fourteen of 9.6 per 100,000, but for the whole state the rate was 54.5. For the whole United States the latter rate was 71.1 per 100,000, considerably above the Sooner figure. Ironically, the substandard houses in the rural areas contributed to the lower rate since they had greater ventilation, which actually reduced the chances of transmission of the tubercle bacilli. Moreover, tuberculosis was always worse in urban states because of the greater population density.[12]

Next to respiratory afflictions, mostly pneumonia, enteric diseases killed most frequently. Typhoid, dysentery, diarrhea, and enteritis accounted for a large portion of the illness and debilitation of children. Diarrhea and enteritis were terms used by the health profession to refer to a range of intestinal illnesses such as salmonellosis, shigellosis, and foodborne illnesses such as botulism and staphylococcal food poisoning.[13] Diarrhea and enteritis as a cause of death in the United States fell dramatically during the thirties, and although Oklahoma experienced the same general decline, it lagged slightly behind. In 1930 the state matched the nation with a crude rate of 18.9 deaths per 100,000; by 1939 the rates were 9.1 and 8.6 with Oklahoma having the larger.

A child eating contaminated fruit in the May Avenue Shacktown, Oklahoma City, 1939. (FSA Collection, Courtesy Library of Congress.)

In 1930 the age-specific death rates for dysentery and typhoid for children under fourteen were 11.2 and 9.6 respectively. Just as diarrhea and enteritis decreased during the decade, so did other enteric diseases. By 1939 death by dysentery was recorded at the rate of 3.5 per 100,000 and typhoid at 2.9.

Records are unavailable on the number of enteric illnesses not ending in death, but it was commonly assumed that children living in areas with poor sewage facilities had dysentery at least once prior to their fifth birthday. Enteric cases were generally higher where "privies" or outdoor toilets were used, especially if they were located near the water supply. On farms waste material from both man and animal often contaminated the water supply. Wherever housing was substandard, whether in town or country, the incidence of enteric diseases was almost always higher. It was for that reason that Oklahoma, where most farms had no running water, had a slightly higher enteric rate, though it was lower than that in some southern states.

CRUDE RATES OF DEATH CAUSED BY DIARRHEA AND ENTERITIS (UNDER TWO YEARS) IN OKLAHOMA AND THE UNITED STATES FOR SELECTED YEARS

YEAR	OKLAHOMA	UNITED STATES
1930	18.9	18.9
1933	17.4	12.5
1937	12.0	11.1
1939	9.1	8.6

Mortality Statistics, 1930, pp. 269, 435; *ibid.*, 1933, pp. 160, 318; *Vital Statistics*, 1937, pp. 28-28; *ibid.*, 1939, pp. 28-29.

Other pronounced differences in Oklahoma health occurred with the common childhood diseases of diphtheria, whooping cough, and measles. Diphtheria had long been a killer of children since 1735 when it killed forty children in Kingston, New Hampshire. In 1890 Emil Von Behring developed an antitoxin for diphtheria which worked successfully as a prophylaxis, and some states and cities, mostly in the Northeast, started immunization programs. Not until 1925 did Oklahoma begin to combat diphtheria and other communicable diseases with the creation of the Bureau of the Communicable Disease Control of Epidemiology. Reduction in the number of deaths was reasonably satisfactory so that by 1930 diphtheria was well in decline. However, the state's slow start meant that death from diphtheria still came at twice the national rate, and the PHS complained about the lack of personnel in the state Bureau, which consisted of one epidemiologist and a part-time clerk. "Very little real control is possible," the PHS reported, and too many county superintendents of health, it added, "know little of public health and have apparently little interest in it."[14]

CRUDE DEATH RATES FOR DIPHTHERIA, WHOOPING COUGH AND SCARLET FEVER 1930, 1935 AND 1940 IN OKLAHOMA AND THE REGISTRATION STATES

YEAR	DIPHTERIA		WHOOPING COUGH		SCARLET FEVER	
	Okla.	U.S.	Okla.	U.S.	Okla.	U.S.
1930	9.0	4.7	6.2	4.8	1.8	1.9
1935	6.0	3.1	6.5	3.7	0.9	2.1
1940	3.0	1.1	2.4	2.2	0.3	0.5

Source: Bureau of the Census, *Vital Statisitics Rates in the United States 1900-1940* (Washington, 1943), pp. 330, 356

Whooping cough, measles, and scarlet fever did not receive as much attention since they struck less frequently, though by the late thirties whooping cough and measles equaled diphtheria as causes of child death. Whooping cough continued to strike owing to the late identification of the bacterium known as pertussis, and because it frequently led to secondary complications such as pneumonia. The higher rate of death from childhood diseases was probably related to the combined conditions of economic hardship, lack of medical care, and the relatively shorter period of time that the state immunization program had been in operation.

CRUDE DEATH RATE FOR MEASLES 1930, 1933 AND 1939 IN OKLAHOMA AND THE UNITED STATES

YEAR	OKLAHOMA	UNITED STATES
1930	4.5	3.1
1933	2.8	2.2
1939	3.1	0.90

Source: *Mortality Statistics 1930*, p. 432; *ibid.*, 1933, p. 315; *Vital Statistics 1939*, p. 304.

The same pattern was true for epidemic poliomyelitis, a childhood disease little understood until the twentieth century. "Few diseases were more feared than polio," wrote one authority, "because it attacked healthy, normal children, leaving many with physical disabilities for the rest of their lives."[15] One of the worst epidemics occurred in New York City in 1916, and as late as the 1920s medical scientists had only fundamental knowledge of the disease. It was a febrile disease of virus origin that usually struck children in the summer months, and man was the only known reservoir. Polio was highly contagious and infected all classes, but

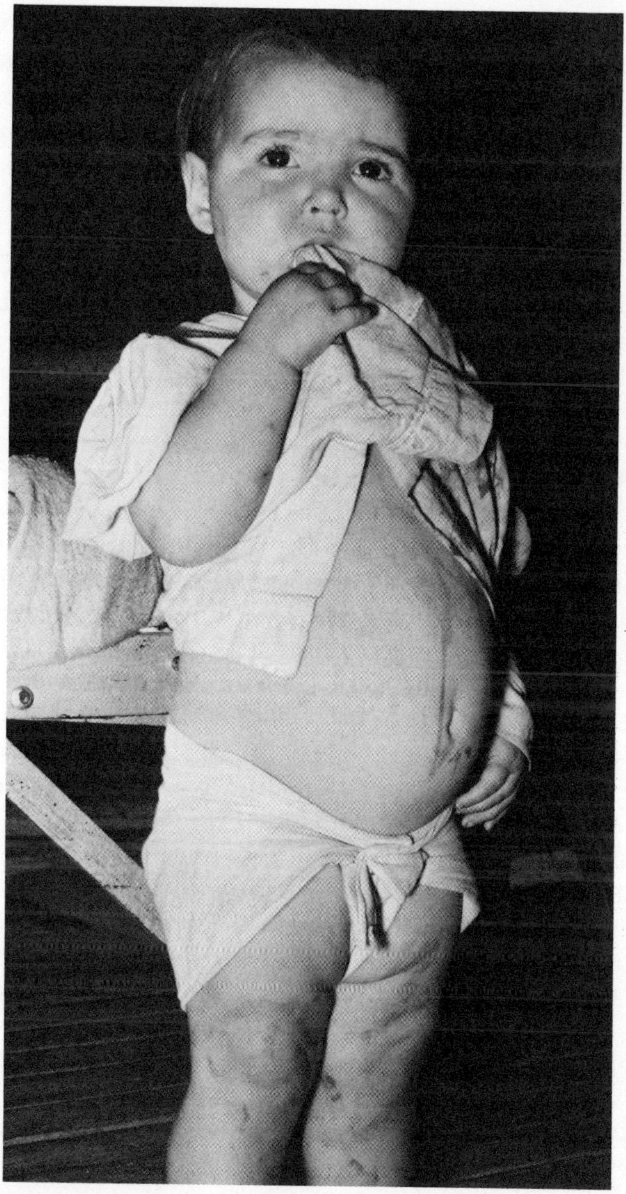

Child with symptoms of malnutrition on farm near Warner, Oklahoma, June, 1939. (FSA Collection. Courtesy Library of Congress.)

showed manifest illness in relatively few persons. No prevention was available and no therapy was effective. Permanent paralysis usually developed in one or more extremities, or death occurred with respiratory failure and circulatory collapse. In 1929 Dr. Philip Drinker of the Harvard School of Public Health introduced the "iron lung" which significantly reduced the rate of death.

As was the case with influenza, Oklahoma had the second highest rate of polio deaths among children fourteen or younger. In 1937 she ranked second to Arkansas in the percentage of all deaths caused by polio. The simple number of deaths for Arkansas was seventy-five. Oklahoma had fifty-four, a high number matched only by Illinois. California recorded fifty-three deaths. Computation of the percentage showed the latter two states were remarkably lower because of their greater population: the percentage of the total deaths for both states caused by polio for children under fourteen was .0006. For Oklahoma it was .0025, and the national average percentage was .0006. Except for their neighbors across the state line in Arkansas, Oklahoma children ran a much greater risk of contracting poliomyelitis. An epidemic may have occurred in 1937 in that two-state area, for the neighboring states of Texas, New Mexico, and Kansas had much lower death rates.[16]

Use of the iron lung was probably negligible except in the most urbanized states since it was a new development. Poorer states had too few artificial respirators and tended, therefore, to have a higher death rate from polio. Periodic outbreaks would not explain the state's greater frequency because it consistently ranked near the top in both simple number of deaths and percentages of total deaths for the years when data were available. The explanation undoubtedly lay in the general lack of health facilities as exemplified by Oklahoma's poor ranking in the quantity of hospital beds per 1,000 population (fifth from bottom) and other indices of health care.[17]

Despite the higher death rates in Oklahoma, frequency of illness would not necessarily be higher since death would occur owing to the lack of sufficient technology to keep patients from reaching the advanced and fatal stages of diseases. For that reason caution must be exercised in using death rates to gauge the incidence of childhood illnesses. In the general population the illness rate was over 100 times the death rate, but children in poorer areas may have experienced a slightly higher loss of life for lack of medical care. The mortality rate could be out of proportion to the morbidity rate, and to the extent this pattern could occur in Oklahoma, children had less chance of surviving.

Two afflictions associated with poverty were pellagra and hookworm; the first was a nutritional deficiency and the other was a parasitic invader. America's first case of pellagra was diagnosed in 1902, and by the thirties its eradication had become a major goal of the PHS. Dr. Joseph Goldberger was chiefly responsible for the anti-pellagra campaign which was centered in the southern states where the malady was endemic. Pellagra caused scaly and crusty skin, loss of weight, poor growth, and could be fatal. Most patients were "prepellagrins," that is, they only reached the intermediate stage of the disease. Because of the characteristics of the disease and its variability related to family income and seasonal weather, only about 10 percent of the cases were reported. So common was the disease in the South, however, that the region was known as the "pellagra belt."[18]

Oklahoma escaped the worst ravages of pellagra which was associated with the institution of share cropping and tenant farming in the South. This institution was visible in the Sooner state, but it never reached comparable proportions. General death rates in Oklahoma for all ages exceeded the national rate throughout the thirties, but fell below the southern states. Children characteristically had a low incidence of the disease, particularly among children under five. In 1930, 300 deaths had occurred in Oklahoma, but only seven victims were under fifteen years of age. For 1937 the PHS reported 107 pellagra deaths, but none occurred among children under fourteen.[19]

Eradication of pellagra began in 1937 when University of Wisconsin scientists discovered its cause—shortage of niacin. Niacin was added to commercially prepared foods such as flour and meal, and by 1945 pellagra had largely disappeared. In common with children throughout the South, Oklahoma children gained some relief from pellagra as they struggled against the deadlier communicable diseases.[20]

Similar to pellagra in its impact and eradication was hookworm, an intestinal parasite that sapped strength and vigor from its host. In 1901 Dr. Bailey K. Ashford discovered hookworm, and further research by PHS officer Charles Stiles and the Rockefeller Foundation in 1908-1913 showed it to be endemic in the southern states. Infestation rates among children averaged 40 percent. Labelled the "American murderer," the hookworm was an insidious creature living on the host's blood, causing loss of energy, weakness, stunted growth, and general anemia. Because death seldom resulted, the Bureau of the Census did not list it as a major cause of death or report infestation rates. Hookworm was nonetheless a major health problem in the South. Rural children were the favorite hosts because of their habits and the necessity of walking barefoot in "polluted soil," the area around the privy and farmyard infested with the hookworm larvae.[21]

It was during the thirties that the greatest progress was made against hookworm. Undoubtedly the most effective contribution came from the Rural Electrification Administration (REA) that went into operation in 1935. The REA enabled farm families to install running water and indoor bathrooms. The REA gave some families special low interest loans for bathroom installations. A privy construction program by the Works Progress Administration (WPA) also improved sanitation. The WPA built or repaired over 62,000 privies in Oklahoma, one of the highest ranking states in this respect. Improved sanitation also reduced illness rates of dysentery, typhoid, and other enteric diseases.[22]

A significant killer of all age groups in the early thirties was malaria, the "ague." Though geographic conditions in

Oklahoma were not as conducive to mosquito-breeding as in some southern states, the southeastern counties nonetheless offered a hospitable environment for these pests. As in the case of pellagra and hookworm, the Sooner State resembled the South in the importance of malaria as a factor in child health, but the disease fortunately never achieved the southern level. Malaria did not match diphtheria and whooping cough as a cause of death, and the rate of infection for children paralleled that of adults. But malaria was more common than infectious diseases; it affected so many persons that industries would not locate near malarial areas, and the recurring fever made its victims highly susceptible to other infections.

Progress toward the eradication of malaria occurred through the home-improvement programs of various federal agencies and the introduction of insecticides, especially DDT in 1939. Conquest of the mosquito during the thirties was related more to the use of window screens, drainage, and the spraying of light petroleum on surface water by health authorities since DDT came too late for the depression years.

COMPARATIVE RATE OF MALARIA DEATHS FOR OKLAHOMA AND THE UNITED STATES

YEAR	U.S.	OKLAHOMA 0-14	OKLAHOMA ADULT
1930	2.9	6.0	6.0
1935	3.5	unavailable	5.8
1940	1.1	1.1	1.3

Source: Bureau of the Census, *Vital Statistics Rates 1900-1940*, pp. 330, 354.

In most respects the mortality and morbidity patterns of Oklahoma children conformed with those of children throughout the United States. Children in other states accounted for a large portion of enteric and communicable diseases. Rheumatism, cerebral hemorrhage, heart disease, and cancer were negligible for children throughout the United States and Oklahoma. The age curve for death and illness showed no difference. Thus, the greatest difference was in the incidence of illness and most specifically the likelihood of early death. The extra burden originated partly from hookworm, pellagra, and malaria, three diseases known as the "scourge of the South." These illnesses were insidious in their effects, and made Oklahoma children more susceptible to other pathogenic invaders, but children in other southern states carried an even heavier burden in this respect. The discrepancy with the nation in infant mortality and rate of death by specific diseases suggested that Oklahoma children, though surviving relatively well as infants, died at a higher rate after their first birthday. In other words, as they contracted potentially fatal diseases, the comparable shortage of facilities, physicians, and other health supportive apparatus reduced their chances of recovery. To the extent that the state's vaccination program was new the death rate was also higher.

Physical defects and impairments were another indication of health. The most common problem for children was dental caries, ranging as high as 65 percent of children examined. Refractive errors ranged from 10 to 25 percent. During the thirties physicians regarded tonsils and adenoids as impediments to health and included them in their examinations. That practice no longer continues, indicating the difficulty of measuring child health in earlier years.[23]

The Oklahoma Department of Public Health conducted examinations of school children and filed reports on the number of children examined and the number having defects. Specific explanations of the defects were not discernible. In 1930, 3,157 school children were examined in Carter County and 1,855 had physical defects, 58.7 percent. For Okmulgee County the percentage was 63.7, and for Seminole County the percentage was 89.4. Without more specific information, comparison of Oklahoma with other states in this respect remains impossible, but it would appear that Sooner children had a slightly higher rate of physical impairments.[24]

Indicative of the anticipated higher rate of defects was the rejection rate of Oklahoma men by the Selective Service during World War II. Poorer states, especially those in the South, had a higher rejection rate, about 50 percent compared with 36 percent of those from other regions according to one study. Oklahoma's rate of rejection for mental illness and musculoskeletal defects surpassed the national average rate, but was the same for hernia and the defects of the eyes. Black registrants fared slightly better in the latter two categories, but significantly outdistanced whites in rejection for mental disease. Syphilis accounted for the highest number of rejections in both races with musculoskeletal causes ranking second. Statistical data reported by the Selective Service were conditioned, of course, by the military's need for manpower which generally grew more demanding through the course of the war. Rejection rates of potential soldiers during the war were, nonetheless, a clear indication of the relative quality of child health in the thirties.[25]

The depression image of Oklahoma as a land of hardship, the center of the dust-bowl, and the origin of migrating "Okies" was reinforced upon examination of the status of child health in the state. When measured against the national pattern of sickness and death, Sooner children had worse health than their contemporaries in three major categories of illnesses: respiratory diseases, enteric diseases, and communicable diseases. In some instances they fared better than children in the South where both economic and geographic conditions, as illustrated by hookworm and pellagra, were even more likely to cause illness, but the overall picture of health in Oklahoma was depressing. The condition was the result of the state's recent entry into the Union and lack of sufficient economic development to provide a strong public health program. The presence of a large

An Oklahoma child on the road in California. Probably suffering from tuberculosis of the bone. (FSA Collection. Courtesy Archives and Records Division, Oklahoma Department of Libraries, Oklahoma City.)

number of rural families living without the advantages of modern housing also accounted for the frequency of pneumonia, the enterides, hookworm, pellagra, and malaria. In the case of tuberculosis, however, the poor housing contributed to lower incidence.

Despite the state's disadvantages, childrens' health improved during the thirties. Improved prevention and treatment came with the continued use of diphtheria antitoxin, the introduction of sulfonamides, the discovery of niacin's anti-pellagra qualities, new techniques for more rapid and exact typing of pneumococci, and the development of specific serums for pneumonia patients.[26] Action by federal and state agencies to combat ill-health as exemplified by the short-lived clinics of the Farm Security Administration and the home improvements wrought by the REA also improved health. Migration into other states reduced the number of Oklahoma's most indigent class, the rural poor. During the thirties Oklahoma lost in net rural population by 117,588 persons, or a decrease of 7.5 percent. The urban population increased 7.1 percent, but a large portion of the rural residents, who experienced most of the state's health problems, left Oklahoma.

Gauging the quality of health could never be free of errors because of the difficulties at the time in obtaining accurate records on deaths and illnesses and the different interpretations of data. Moreover, published records tended to understate rates; however, available information and the records of men rejected by the Selective Service make it obvious that medical hardship in Oklahoma during the Great Depression reached a dimension previously unrecognized.

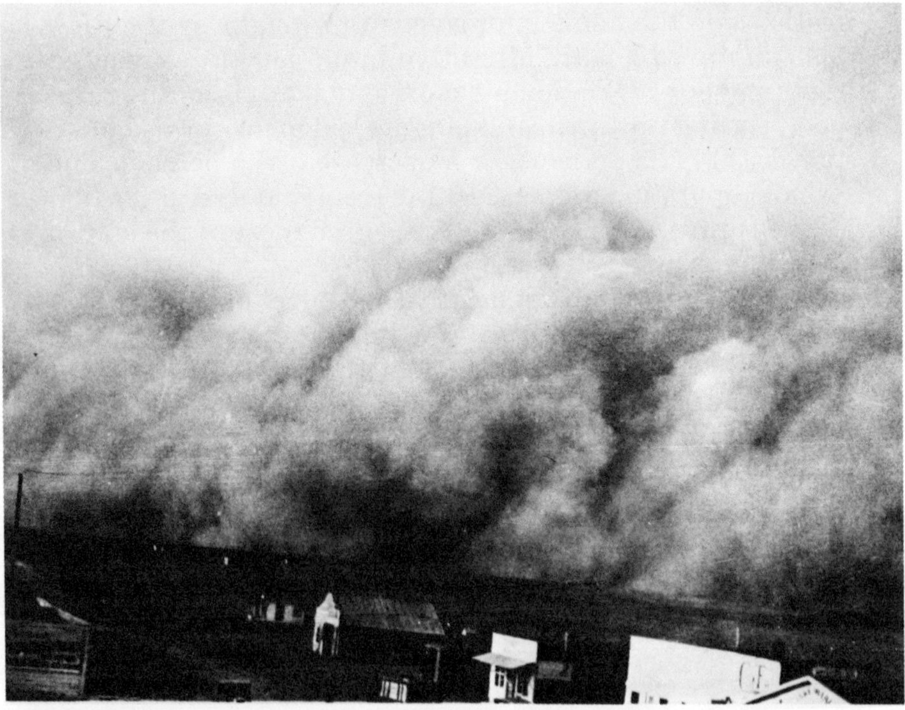

Duststorm approaching Knowles, Oklahoma, 1935. (Courtesy Western History Collections, University of Oklahoma Library.)

Dust, Farmers, and the Federal Government

By C. Roger Lambert

The combined effects of depression and drought in the 1930s brought to Oklahoma a sort of fame the state has since rarely equalled. The image was of 'Okies,' a term attached to those migrants who moved out of the drought and depression plagued region far beyond the state's borders. Art, literature, music, and film all portrayed the devastation of the region. Scholars talked of the "Desert Threat" and government offcials, journalists, and others warned that the western part of the state must be returned to grassland and much of the population moved elsewhere to avoid total disaster. Some were convinced that it was already too late. Man had cultivated land that should never have been plowed; blowing dust then removed the fertile topsoil. The results, some feared, were that man had destroyed in one generation what nature took millions of years to create.[1]

Although Oklahoma farmers experienced the same kind of growth and technical development in the period after

1914 as other American farmers, the conditions of life remained "well below the norm" of other Americans.[2] Farmers suffered from surpluses, low prices, excessive debts, and high costs through the 1920s. All of these continued and rapidly worsened as the Great Depression developed. Despite the efforts of President Herbert Hoover's Federal Farm Board, cotton and wheat prices fell to disastrous levels. The decline in price of the two major crops was only symptomatic of the effects of the depression which produced an overall decline of almost 64 percent in farm income.[3]

As the depression worsened and the drought of 1930 developed, the condition of Oklahoma farmers rapidly grew more serious. The 1930 drought hit more than twenty states, but it centered in the east rather than the plains area. By the fall state leaders in Oklahoma feared that farmers would be forced to dispose of their breeding stock because of feed shortages and lack of money. In early September 500 farmers in Latimer County passed a resolution requesting aid, and they reported that a survey showed that six out of seven families in the rural section of the county would need assistance.

Oklahoma was the first state to receive federal drought money for loans to farmers, and the drought organization of the state provided the model for the other states. The southwest corner of the state reported that hundreds of farmers were in "immediate need for food for their families, feed for their farm horses and cattle, seed wheat" and coal for the winter. The idea of federal drought aid for seed and feed was not such a blow to tradition as that of providing food for humans. The food relief issue became involved with the issue of national unemployment relief. It brought a bitter and prolonged debate between Congress and President Herbert Hoover and set the tone of the relief controversy for the next three years. Congress appropriated some $65 million which could be used for all types of drought relief. Additionally, the Red Cross became extensively involved in providing food aid.[4] The 1930 drought was only a rehearsal for the great drought to come in mid-decade. In every respect the later drought caused far greater suffering and devastation, but in the meantime the federal government became more accustomed to massive aid programs, and the people came to expect more federal assistance.

Drought, depression, and the inactivity of the Hoover Administration brought a degree of radicalism to Oklahoma between 1930 and 1933. Mrs. R. D. Rood, National Committeewoman of the Republican Party in Oklahoma, protested that No. 1 hard wheat was selling for only twenty-seven cents on the farm and warned about the "active hostility and opposition of the people." John A. Simpson, President of the Farmers Union, the most radical of the major farm organizations, became more vocal, charging that the "capitalistic system is of the devil's making" and advocating cost of production as the only method for farm relief. By 1932 Senator Elmer Thomas was much concerned about mortgage foreclosure and insisted that there was no way the eastern insurance companies gaining ownership of Oklahoma farmland could be beneficial to the state. He co-sponsored a bill "to Abolish the Federal Farm Board and Secure to the Farmers the Cost of Production."[5]

Thomas merely reflected the views he heard from home. As one unhappy farmer complained, people were "getting disgusted" as Congress seemed to have plenty of money "to paint a picture of President Coolidge, money to catch the kidnapers, plenty of money for the Banks. . . and only hell for the poor hungry farmers." In late March 1933 another pointed out that the dust was blowing and that the soil was "blown off as deep as it has been plowed." He warned that the next cry from the farmer would be "give us equality or give us death. . . . We want equality and sooner or later we are going to have it . . . with the people losing this year's wheat crop and no living price. . . . We are going to be face to face with starvation all over the Panhandle country." He concluded with the warning: "Capital may think they have the common people cowed and that they won't rebel, but so did England think at one time." Agricultural fundamentalism was clearly expressed by another who warned: "Destroy the farmers, the men, the women of this nation or any nation that till the soil and you destroy civilization. Will we right the old ship of state before it's to[o] late or go down never to rise again?" As the New Deal of Franklin Delano Roosevelt replaced the Hoover Administration the radicalism abated. While Congress debated the Agricultural Adjustment Act in the spring of 1933, a farmer wrote to Thomas: "Your name will be among those voting yes or there won't be any barbecue when you come home."[6]

The farm legislation passed and the Roosevelt Administration, far more eager than its predecessor to assist the needy farmers, moved quickly through the AAA to implement production control and to get money into the hands of farmers with a cotton plow-up and the Emergency Hog Marketing Act. The plan to buy pregnant sows and little pigs brought great controversy. The hogs under eighty-one pounds in weight were too small for the processing equipment, and it was planned to turn them into tankage. The processors were flooded with small pigs since the government was paying up to double their market value. Quickly stories about little pig bodies floating down the rivers covered the country and protests about the nature of the program and the waste of good food developed. In Oklahoma many also complained that the packers and speculators were the only people to benefit from the purchases. Senator Thomas P. Gore protested that there were grounds to "debate this whole policy of murdering pigs . . . but certainly if . . . the taxpayers are going to pay twice what they are worth, the farmer who owns the pigs ought to get the benefits." Gore concluded that he did not consider that the "butchery of these pigs is as bad as the slaying of Rachel's children by Herod of Old." While Gore implied some concern about the moral issues of the slaughter, he was essentially concerned that so many farmers complained they were unable to sell hogs while the speculators were able to sell any number they wished. A farmer charged that "The Pig

Deal makes the Infamous Tea Pot Dome Oil deal smell like a bed of roses." A more significant complaint was the one voiced by D. P. Trent, Director of Extension Service at Stillwater, Oklahoma, who denied that there was a surplus of hogs "on the farms of Oklahoma as long as the children in 50,000 to 60,000 farm homes of the state are hungry for meat most of the year." Trent urged distribution of the live hogs to needy farmers "which have no hogs whatever, and which do without meat most of the year. . . ."[7] Distribution of live hogs would have limited or destroyed the production control element of the purchase and was not considered. The other complaints were in part legitimate but were difficult to control and were not sufficiently serious to negate the relief aspect of the program. This purchase, as much as anything the AAA did, indicated the new and more activist policy the federal government would follow in the much greater disaster that was already looming over the state.

One subordinate element in the hog purchases involved drought relief and was of considerable value to Oklahoma. In the twenties Oklahoma recorded rainfall "far above normal." Although 1930 reminded people of the danger of drought, 1931 was a good year and farmers forgot about drought in their joy over good crops and their dismay over low prices. Part of the state received less than half of normal rainfall in 1932 and tax delinquency and mortgage foreclosures became common. A group in Hughes County met to discuss the situation and adopted the slogan "We'll stick tighter than a cocklebur in a mule's tail." In 1933, when dust storms began in January and continued steadily through July, the mule's tail became somewhat loose. Sand blew so thick that people lost their way, hens went to roost at midday, lights burned all day without great effect, airports closed, and trains slowed to a crawl or stopped. In at least one case, police blocked the roads to prevent dangerous travel. Livestock and humans suffered from a variety of lung disorders.[8]

Just as the drought made agriculture a more perilous venture than usual, the economic depression sent people back to the land. D. P. Trent, Oklahoma extension director, estimated that some 7,833 unemployed families settled on vacant farms in the state in 1932, in a kind of forerunner of the homestead and resettlement ventures under the New Deal. Unfortunately, most of these people were ill-equipped in both training and resources to make a success of farming, and the drought only made failure more likely. Demonstrating another misplaced confidence was an effort to encourage farmers and others to grow their own food. A number of county governments joined women's clubs and charity groups in early 1933 to encourage the planting of emergency gardens. They distributed seeds and plowed up vacant lots for garden space and urged all farmers to grow as much of their own food as possible.[9]

As drought continued into mid-summer many of the gardens wilted and government experts began to talk of massive crop failure as a distinct possibility. In response to the situation there was a conference in Guymon to consider conditions. A Texas reporter gave a devastating description:

> Not a blade of wheat in Cimarron County, Oklahoma; Cattle dying there on the range; A few bushels of wheat in the Perryton area against an average yield of from four to six million bushels;... sixty cattle dying Friday afternoon between Guymon and Liberal from some disease induced by dust—humans suffering from dust fever.

This conference of drought victims was followed by a meeting of governors from drought states; and both groups asked for relief assistance.[10] Although 1933 offered a severe challenge to farmers, most reacted with traditional hope saying "all we need is a little bit of rain,"[11] but that confidence was backed with cotton money and hog purchase money from the AAA and with job relief from the Civilian Conservation Corps and the Federal Emergency Relief Administration. More normal rain during the late summer of 1933 added to the confidence but left the farmer ill-prepared for the much more severe drought of 1934.

In 1934, drought covered virtually the entire country west of the Mississippi River. Intense dry and hot weather hit first in the northern plains and spread gradually to the south and west. As summer came to Oklahoma the same problems developed as in the previous year, but with greater intensity. In July the state set new records almost daily for high temperatures and the longest period without any rainfall. The state experienced some eighty-three days of over 100-degree temperatures with a high of 116 degrees. Although the dust storms were not as severe as the year before, they nevertheless occurred with alarming intensity. One Oklahoman said after breathing the sand-laden air: "Ah: we can not only breathe the air of liberty but we can eat it as well."[12]

By July, Texas, Beaver, Cimarron, and Harper counties in the western region were described as a mere desert of sand. Livestock and humans suffered from heat and some deaths were reported. Farmers hauled water up to twenty miles in an attempt to save their stock. Others drove livestock as far as ten miles to water. Crops were reported as almost a total failure and most gardens were in severe trouble with reports that garden stuff had simply cooked in the ground. Springs never known to cease running were completely dry. In August hogs were reported dead from lack of food and one farmer near Talala declared that he was willing to give away some 100 hogs and would even help load them if anyone would take them so that he would not have to watch them starve to death.[13] W. L. Evans, who farmed southeast of Muskogee, summarized the situation faced by Oklahoma farmers:[14]

> I have lived on the same farm for 46 years and in Muskogee County for 55 years this [sic] is the first season that I had to call for help. My 133 head of cattle will need winter feed and I don't know where its coming from. I raised six tons of hay and 15 tons of darso; ordinarily I raise 45 to 50 tons of grain sorghums and 30 tons of hay. My corn crop

> on 20 acres will not make more than 50 bushels. Plenty of water from mountain streams but pastures are gone.

This farmer was much better off than many in the state because he produced some feed and still had water. The concern about what do for the winter and the necessity for outside assistance described the state of many Oklahoma farmers.

After a decade of depressed agricultural prices, a major depression now in its fourth year, and the third year out of four with serious drought conditions, Oklahoma was unprepared to meet the new disaster without outside assistance. State officials, farm groups, and Department of Agriculture representatives all agreed on the need which was essentially a national need. The New Deal prepared to meet the crisis with a wide variety of assistance programs to

An abandoned farm near Newport, Oklahoma, 1937. (Courtesy Western History Collections, University of Oklahoma Library.)

provide both immediate relief and long term reform. Of the relief programs the more traditional involved the expansion of the already existing loan programs, permission for those farmers who had contracted to withdraw some of their acreage from production to plant forage or feed crops, the reduction of rail rates for shipping feed into the area and shipping livestock out to pasture, and work relief. Authorities also ordered an immediate expansion of such work programs as road construction and conservation activities such as dam construction and well digging. Such organizations as the CCC and FERA were authorized to expand their employment, particularly in those areas most severely affected by drought.[15]

The most impressive of the relief measures was the effort to save the cattle industry. The AAA planners felt that the cattle surplus constituted the primary long-term problem for the industry and had tried for more than a year to get the cattlemen to agree to a production control program. However, not until the farmers experienced a disastrous drop in prices in the winter of 1933 followed by the drought did the planners get their desire. Late in May the AAA began buying cattle in the northern plains to save them from starvation. This was the beginning of a purchase program that would last eight months and would remove nearly 8.3 million cattle.[16]

The drought relief program for cattlemen involved a twofold classification system. As drought officials decided that conditions merited, counties were declared either emergency, where all relief activities including the federal purchase of cattle were implemented, or secondary, which brought all relief except federal buying. The purchase process was relatively simple with government agents and Animal Bureau inspectors buying the animals on the farm. The seller received a contract which required him to cooperate in future production control programs. He then received a purchase payment and a benefit payment. The purchase price was subject to the claims of lien holders but the benefit payment was reserved for the owner. The government paid from $6.00 to $14.00 for cattle over two years old, from $5.00 to $10.00 for younger cattle, and from $1.00 to $5.00 for calves. The benefit payment ranged from $3.00 to $6.00. In Oklahoma the average payment was $12.10.[17]

Although Oklahoma did not suffer the extreme drought of the northern plains in the spring of 1934, the state received barely half its normal rainfall after May and by the end of August all seventy-seven counties in the state were designated as emergency areas with extreme drought conditions. As the federal activities developed in Oklahoma purchases came quickly. On January 1, 1933, BAE experts estimated the total cattle population in the state at 2,464,000. Drought purchases reached approximately 503,480, of which some 42 percent, as against a national average of about 18 percent, were condemned as unfit for human consumption. Drought-purchased cattle were segregated as to their acceptability for food. Those accepted were turned over to the Federal Surplus Relief Corporation to be processed for relief food. Those condemned were destroyed, usually shot and buried, on the farm. Even these were available for use by the family and, at times, other needy individuals.[18]

The lowest average price of all range states and the highest number of condemned cattle reflected the extent of suffering in Oklahoma. The federal payment of almost five and three-quarters million dollars for cattle provided considerable benefit to the state but represented only a small part of what the state received from federal support. A related activity was the establishment of canneries to process the beef. Following a model established in Texas in 1933, these were put into operation in strategic places throughout the state. In addition to the beef provided to the needy, the plants provided several thousand jobs which went in good part to needy farmers. Additional jobs were developed under the CCC and the FERA to get the stricken farmers through the year.[19] Temporary relief work and free beef from the canning projects offered immediate survival but did not meet the long-term needs of Oklahoma farmers.

A rural housing survey by the Extension Service suggested the degree of need among farmers. At least one farm home out of eight was in such condition that building a new house was preferable to repairs. At least one-third of the homes needed to be increased in size by one or more bedrooms. Over 60 percent of the houses needed roof repairs, and nearly 45 percent were in need of foundation work. Over 71 percent needed repairs of some type.[20] Abandoned and deserted homesteads were all that remained of once prosperous efforts. This process of abandonment increased at an alarming rate during the next two years.

Oklahoma, receiving extensive federal aid, survived 1934 and many expected to see a return to more normal rainfall in 1935. Disappointment came quickly. Although drought was not nearly so serious, the dust returned with a vengeance. Soon observers were declaring that each duster was the worst yet. Clouds of dust again closed schools, reduced visibility—at least once to zero—made upper lung disorders worse, contributed to or caused a number of deaths, both animal and human, and killed countless fish as streams and ponds heated and dried. The spring months were the worst for drought and dust but unlike previous years the dusters continued on into the fall and winter. There was even a severe dust storm in mid-December.[21]

Strange stories appeared such as that of the jackrabbit which came into a farmyard obviously sick and injured by the wind and dust. He stayed around to be cleaned, doctored and fed, and he left only when well. Farm youths reported that they had never found rabbit hunting so easy as they could simply walk up to the animals and kill them with a club. Others reported that after dust storms they had to wash the eyes of their chickens. There was a form of graveyard humor which sought to keep up the courage. "Knock, knock" jokes attached themselves to the drought. A traveler "reported seeing a prairie dog 100 feet in the air, burrowing."[22] Most farmers seemed to resent attacks upon the region, and continued to preface almost every statement with the phrase "if it rains."

Although some observers described 1935 as the worst year of the drought in Oklahoma, 1936 presented a strong challenge for that honor. In the first three and one-half months the state received only 20 percent of its normal rainfall. The dry and extremely hot weather covered virtually the entire state. A federal agent for the WPA in mid-July reported on conditions in Oklahoma. Temperatures had been "ranging from 100 to 120" and people were "hauling drinking water for miles and miles." The Resettlement Director in the state claimed needs that the agent found "absurd." Of 213,000 farm families, Oklahoma authorities estimated that up to 70,000 would need relief. In reality, the total would later go up to 100,000 families. Crop production declined by 50 to 60 percent compared to 1935, and farmers produced only two percent of the 1935 peach crop. From eastern Oklahoma it

A truck buried in dust, Cimarron County. (Courtesy Western History Collections, University of Oklahoma Library)

was reported that the cotton crop had failed so completely that farmers would not have cotton stalks to see their cattle through the winter.[23] The drought was more severe in 1936 but the dust storms lessened. Drought and dust continued into 1937 and 1938 but with less intensity. Crop production gradually increased and with it hope. By 1939 experts proclaimed that the Dust Bowl had been expelled from Oklahoma.[24]

As drought and disaster continued into the mid and late thirties, more extreme proposals developed for solutions. Some farmers proposed that the federal government establish martial law and others wanted the President to appoint a dictator who would have the power to do anything and everything necessary to end the dust. Others issued veiled threats to neighbors who refused to keep their fields in condition to prevent it from blowing. One scholar developed a plan to cover the plains with plaster of paris which would prevent blowing and preserve moisture so that farming could continue. Others discussed depopulation of the entire western third of the state—with the exception of the urban areas. This was not a new idea but now F. L. Vaughn, secretary of the state Conservation Commission, declared that conservation officials agreed that the region "never could be reclaimed as long as private land owners remain on it."[25] Farmers responded "no" to this idea. They insisted that this was "old stuff" remembering a similar plan urged by Secretary of the Interior Harold Ickes back in 1933. There was a simpler way to solve the drought problems, said Henry A. Long of Guymon. "Give us," he urged, "some more . . . rain." Long also expressed doubt that the farmers could move as "they have been dry out here so long I'm afraid they wouldn't take root anywhere else."[26]

The spirited rejection of evacuation was admirable, but there was an out-migration as early as 1933. Since this movement conflicted with the efforts of the government and the effects of the depression, a number of agencies sought to resettle unemployed and displaced farmers on the land. Some officials viewed this as the only way to get people off the relief rolls. Although the idea had a few merits, it was clear that these new farmers would probably remain at the subsistence level. In 1936 the state WPA administrator urged a drive to place approximately 43,000 farmers from the relief rolls on farms where they would join nearly 72,000 others who had moved back to the land since 1930.[27] Significantly, the largest gains were in the eastern region of the state where 70 to 80 percent of the farmers were tenants, compared to a statewide average of 62 percent.[28]

A federal official reported that he met ten loaded trucks moving toward Arkansas where the people hoped to "at least raise a garden and have fuel." When it was first suggested that people should leave the worst drought regions, there was an angry protest. In 1934 some left quietly and in 1935 they were leaving in such numbers that it was clearly noticeable. Although over 71,000 people moved back to the farm in the first half of the thirties the state apparently lost around 30,000 farmers. The large movement to California and the West did not become noticeable until 1935. Significantly, a large part of these seem to have come from the eastern part of Oklahoma, that is, the area of high farm tenancy. The drought played a part in the out-migration, but federal programs which permitted cotton farmers to get rid of their tenants obviously played a greater role since many of those who left came from the region devastated least by the drought. While some of the experts, including federal agents, supported the idea of removing large numbers from the dry area, this was not politically possible. Roosevelt in 1936 told the country that: "It was their fathers' task to make homes; it is their task to keep those homes; it is our task to help them with their fight."[29]

Roosevelt rejected the extreme solutions and concentrated on the revival of the devastated region. In the midst of the drought he proposed the slogan "A Pond for Every Farmer" be used in Oklahoma.[30] He wanted to create an atmosphere of hope to replace that of fear and frustration. Instead of a Dust Bowl dictator, he appointed a coordinator and created a Great Plains Committee to recommend long term solutions for the region. Some of the impetus for planning came from Rexford Tugwell, head of the Resettlement Administration. He wrote Roosevelt in late 1935 that "a large percentage of the population" in the drought area was now on the rolls for relief and, he suggested, "will remain there." The government efforts had reduced the blowing situation but the return was not in proportion to the outlay. "It costs enough to protect uncovered land for two years to buy it," he urged. Tugwell wanted to apply pressure through the AAA, the states, and the Soil Conservation Service to limit farming and buy "the worst lands."[31]

Both the Great Plains Drought Area Committee and the Committee on the Future of the Great Plains suggested that federal acquisition of land, resettlement out of the region, and enlargement of farm size would help the area. Although the reports indicated other possible remedies such as water resources development, irrigation, limiting stock, and returning plowed lands to grass, the limitation of population and the federal acquisition of land for restoration with the more careful use of grazing of range probably led the suggestions for the reformation of agriculture in the drought region.[32] Although these study groups all tended to support some form of regional planning and, perhaps, significant restructuring of life in the drought region, such major development did not come.

Instead the Resettlement Administrators helped some people move out of the region, while they fed, housed, and cared for others. The Works Progress Administration and the CCC provided work relief. Various federal agencies provided loans. Some limited acreage was acquired by federal authorities who hoped to demonstrate what good management could do to revive the land. Other acquired land was turned into game preserves and recreational areas.

In August and September of 1936 Roosevelt toured some of the drought regions (not Oklahoma) and met with representatives from the drought states. The Oklahoma delegation presented the President with an extensive plan for relief and reclamation of the state which would cost up to

$31 million. Governor E. W. Marland told the President that 18,000 Oklahomans were on resettlement grants, between 19,000 and 22,000 on drought aid, and that he wished to add 75,000 to 100,000 farm families to the work relief rolls. As Roosevelt recognized, that would mean over 40 percent of the farmers of Oklahoma receiving federal assistance. Marland wanted the federal government to put them to work "building ponds, dams and terracing." He urged that a pond be built on every farm and he proposed building a larger lake in each of the seventy-seven counties. Roosevelt pointed out that in other states such assistance had been essentially in the form of demonstration with the farmer giving an easement for public purposes to the government. Marland insisted that Oklahoma could not do much on its own and that many farmers would not give easements that would permit public usage.[33]

Essentially Oklahoma wanted federal aid without making much, if any, contribution. Federal authorities had already discovered how essential it was to push the state and the people into making some effort. The conference was somewhat inconclusive with Roosevelt indicating that assistance could be obtained, but that easements and some state action would be necessary. Grudgingly the state legislature responded by providing some funds. A pond building program began and there was even some terracing before the end of the decade. An indication of achievement occurred in Beaver County, where farmers built 180 ponds between 1936 and 1939 with others projected for 1940.[34]

More significant than the construction of ponds was the effort to teach farmers better methods. Although many farmers knew how to farm in semi-arid areas, they tended to neglect that knowledge after 1914. The Soil Erosion Service, located in the Department of the Interior, began even before the drought to encourage farmers in better techniques. After 1933 the SES launched demonstration projects showing the value of dry-land farming using rotation, drought resistant crops, terracing, contouring, listing, and strip cropping, quickly demonstrating that such methods resulted in higher productivity. As the drought continued and the Department of Agriculture became more involved in helping the farmer, the SES was moved over to that department and joined with other conservation agencies to form the Soil Conservation Service. The SCS expanded on what was already under way, working with soil conservation districts that were organized on the local level. By 1939 Oklahoma boasted that it had a larger number of such districts than any state. With its demonstration plots showing 50 percent and at times even more increase in productivity, the SCS offered a major inducement to farmers to follow better methods. Additional inducements were provided in the way of cash and withholding of money under Agricultural Adjustment contracts.[35]

Before the end of the decade farmers were bragging about their "high gear" and other drought resistant crops. Others pointed to the significant increase in productivity using the conservation methods. Farm holdings increased significantly in size. Following the prompting of the federal agents, cattle numbers were down almost a quarter of a million below the 1933 figure.[36] Production in all major crops was returning to previous levels partially as a result of better methods, but also because of the return of more favorable weather. In spite of improved conditions, Clarence Roberts, editor of the *Farmer Stockman*, warned in 1940 that it was time to "start saving the soil." The farmer, he urged, cannot rely on or wait for the government to save him. Roberts argued that title to land did not confer upon the individual the right to "so use or neglect the soil that it will be destroyed."[37] Roberts realized what some of the farmers did not.

Government relief and government guidance helped the farmers survive the desperate decade. Farmers moved under extreme pressure to rectify some of their worst methods but that did not signify a basic change in values. Most importantly, as 1940 came so did a return to above-normal rain which would continue through the next five years. And with the greatly increased demand for farm products brought by World War II, prices for their crops increased. Sadly, many farmers lapsed into the same dangerous practices as before 1934, but the return of serious drought conditions at the end of the forties found Oklahoma farmers better able to withstand the threat. Farms were larger, farmers had the equipment for dry-land farming, and stock ponds helped with water problems for cattlemen.

Hard Times in Oklahoma:

A Photographic Essay

Compiled by Kenneth E. Hendrickson, Jr.

A graphic scene of dustbowl devastation. Farm machinery buried by blowing dust in Cimarron County, April, 1936. Photograph by Arthur Rothstein for the Farm Security Administration. (Courtesy Library of Congress.)

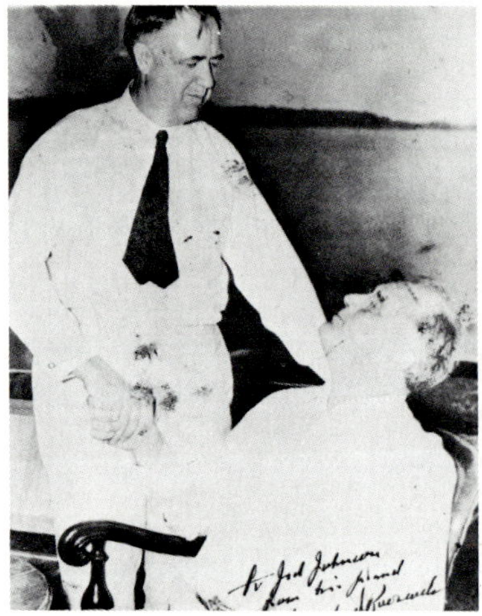

Congressman Jed Johnson with President Roosevelt. (Courtesy Western History Collections, University of Oklahoma Library.)

The old 101 Ranch store. This building housed the offices of the National Youth Administration and the Farm Security Administration. It also contained a dormitory for boys. (Courtesy Western History Collections, University of Oklahoma Library.)

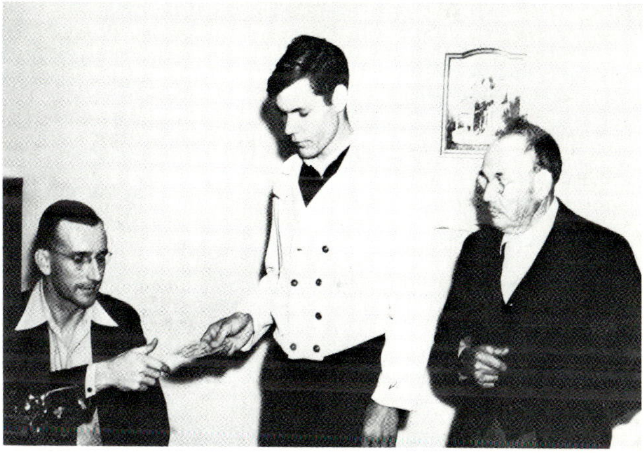

(Above) Director William H. Robertson (left) accepts Carl S. Fawcett into the National Youth Administration farm project at the 101 Ranch near Ponca City. On the right is Carl's grandfather, John R. Ash. (Courtesy Western History Collections, University of Oklahoma Library.)

(Left) President Franklin Delano Roosevelt speaks from the back of a train in Oklahoma with Congressman Lyle Boren on his right and son Elliott on his left. (Courtesy Western History Collections, University of Oklahoma Library.)

The NYA boys on the 101 Ranch hitched up the regular farm team to an old-time prairie schooner and entered the Pioneer Day Parade. Notice the water barrel tied on and the reversed sign which reads "Strip or Bust." They were portraying pioneers who took part in the Cherokee Strip opening in 1893. (Courtesy Western History Collections, University of Oklahoma Library.)

A scene from the Red River Toll Bridge dispute at the Oklahoma end of the Denison Bridge. Governor Murray confers with the National Guard, 1931. (Courtesy Western History Collections, University of Oklahoma Library.)

Dust was not the only hindrance to transportation. This road in McIntosh County became a quagmire when it rained. Photograph by Russell Lee for the Farm Security Administration, February, 1940. (Courtesy Library of Congress.)

(Below) Dust surrounds a farmhouse in western Oklahoma. Photograph by Arthur Rothstein for the Farm Security Administration, April, 1936. (Courtesy Library of Congress.)

A meeting of the Worker's Alliance in Muskogee. Photograph by Russell Lee for the Farm Security Administration, July, 1939. (Courtesy Library of Congress.)

(Below) Residents of the May Avenue agricultural workers' camp in Oklahoma City. Photograph by Russell Lee for the Farm Security Administration, July, 1939. (Courtesy Library of Congress.)

A mother and her children in the agricultural worker's shacktown at Elm Grove. Photograph by Dorothea Lange, August, 1936. (Courtesy Library of Congress.)

Stanley Clark, an old-time Oklahoma Socialist, addresses a meeting of the Workers' Alliance in Muskogee. Photograph for the Farm Security Administration, July, 1939. (Courtesy Library of Congress.)

(Above) A tenant farmer returning home from market in Muskogee. Photograph by Russell Lee for the Farm Security Administration, July, 1939. (Courtesy Library of Congress.)

A tenant farmer and his wife at their home near Warner. Photograph by Russell Lee for the Farm Security Administration, June, 1939. (Courtesy Library of Congress.)

(Top) A crossroads country store in McIntosh County. Photograph by Russell Lee for the Farm Security Administration, June, 1939. (Courtesy Library of Congress.)

(Bottom) A street scene in Slick, Oklahoma, an oil ghost town. Photograph by Russell Lee for the Farm Security Administration, 1940. (Courtesy Library of Congress.)

Main Street in Oklahoma City. All the buildings pictured have since been demolished. Photograph by John Vachon for the Farm Security Administration, November, 1942. (Courtesy Library of Congress.)

A street scene in Sallisaw. Photograph by Dorothea Lange. August, 1936. (Courtesy Library of Congress.)

(Below) Choppy Poafpybitty and her children at Cache Creek Mission west of Apache. (Courtesy Western History Collections, University of Oklahoma Library.)

(Above) An Indian boy and his ancestors. This young Cherokee boy, son of tenant farmers, stands on an iron bed posed between elaborately framed portraits of his forebearers in happier days. The farm was located near Sallisaw. Photograph by Russell Lee for the Farm Security Administration. 1939. (Courtesy Library of Congress and the University of Tulsa.)

Impoverished Indian tenant farmers in their McIntosh County home. Notice the wallpaper fashioned from the covers of magazines such as Capper's Farmer, Woman's World *and others. Photograph by Russell Lee for the Farm Security Administration, probably 1939. (Courtesy Library of Congress and the University of Tulsa.)*

In the 1920s and 1930s it was common for western Oklahoma Indian women to wear traditional blankets over white fashioned dresses. Pictured here are Mrs. Yellowfish and her daughter Faye, the wife of Albert Attocknie, with children. (Courtesy Western History Collections, University of Oklahoma Library.)

Two young Kiowa girls have put on traditional dress for the photographer. (Courtesy Western History Collections, University of Oklahoma Library.)

Elegance and dignity of Kiowa Indian dress are apparent in this photograph of the Apekaum sisters. Alice (right) and Emma (left) were granddaughters of the Kiowa Chief Stumbling Bear. Among the first girls in their tribe to receive white people's education, as adults they were social leaders in both Indian and white culture. They were eloquent speakers in both Kiowa and English. (Courtesy Western History Collections, University of Oklahoma Library.)

"We've Got the Hoover Blues": Oklahoma Transiency in the Days of the Great Depression

By Donald W. Whisenhunt

Transiency was a major social characteristic of the Great Depression, but it is one of the least studied social phenomena of that remarkable decade. The fact that the transient represented the most significant human suffering and misery may well have contributed to the unpopularity of the subject among scholars. Furthermore, those people who moved from place to place were among the most inarticulate of Americans; very few of them left written records, and the records that exist from that era are sometimes not very useful. Even oral history available today from former depression transients is not very helpful, either because of faulty memory, a desire not to recall unpleasant experiences, or the problem of selective memories that sometimes romanticize the transient life.

Transiency in Oklahoma is even more difficult to define. To speak of "Okies" in the thirties immediately conjures up the image portrayed by John Steinbeck in *The Grapes of Wrath*. Any study of Oklahoma transiency in the thirties must, without question, deal with this significant social movement, but there are other elements of transiency that must also be recognized.

The Joads in *The Grapes of Wrath* were forced to move partially because of the dust storms that became serious in the plains states in the thirties. A close reading of the book reveals, however, that they moved for several other reasons as well. Even so, the term "Dust Bowl" has entered the American vocabulary and remains today. A catchy phrase, it is misleading, if not actually incorrect as recent scholarship reveals. One student contended that the popular conception of "Okies" and their migration "needs careful and methodical overhaul, and should be placed forever in the graveyard of American mythology."[1] Oklahomans were, in fact, moving off their farms even before the new wave of dust storms; this freak of nature got media attention and made the "Dust Bowl" a famous and enduring phrase.[2]

The "Dust Bowl" as popularly perceived affected a relatively small portion of Oklahoma. The dust storms brought by the extended drought of the thirties covered western Kansas, the Texas Panhandle, eastern Colorado and eastern New Mexico as well as the Panhandle of Oklahoma. The Oklahoma area affected—the plains constituting the six northwestern counties—was a relatively small portion of the state. Without question, drought and dust storms caused many people to leave the farms, but many other reasons can also be cited. The Dust Bowl was not the real reason for migration.[3]

Oklahoma, like most states of the South and Southwest, had its share of outsiders moving through in search of work. Since massive unemployment affected all of the United States—most seriously impacting the industrial states—surplus workers took to the road seeking employment. In many instances, job seekers took their wives and children with them rather than to break up the family. These family groups walked, hitchhiked, and rode freight trains in their travels. Quite a large number of people, some of them mere children, travelled alone. Transients coming into Oklahoma, whether alone or in family groups, were no more welcome than they were in other southwestern states.[4]

People of diverse backgrounds moved through Oklahoma. For example, a Catholic priest from Pittsburgh, Pennsylvania, came through Oklahoma in 1932 seeking votes in his futile presidential campaign. Father James R. Cox was the candidate of a minor political organization known as the Jobless Party. His vice presidential candidate was Dr. V. C. Tisdal of Elk City, Oklahoma. Cox and a small campaign staff visited Dr. Tisdal in September 1932 while on a campaign swing to California. Cox was not a typical transient of the thirties, but he was one of many people moving through Oklahoma. It is true, nonetheless, that his campaign party was almost without funds and on at least one occasion, had to call on Dr. Tisdal for financial assistance in order to continue the journey.[5]

The people moving through the state were of all types, including pregnant women travelling alone. In 1933 a pregnant woman from Bolinger, Alabama, tried to get to her sister's home in Clovis, New Mexico, before her baby was born. Although she was able to get through Oklahoma she did not make it to New Mexico in time. According to press reports, she gave birth to a son in a railroad freight car in Dalhart, Texas. The newspaper called the baby "'Hobo Bill', five-day old knight of the box car."[6] Although it is impossible to document conclusively, it is reasonable to assume that this type of thing occurred regularly within Oklahoma.

The intrastate movement of people is another element of transiency that must be recognized in Oklahoma in the thirties. A recent study revealed that transiency, a characteristic of the Oklahoma farm economy long before the depression, was merely intensified by hard times nationwide.[7] An examination of instate migrants is complicated, however, by the difficulty of determining if the transients were native Oklahomans or nonresidents seeking employment in Oklahoma or elsewhere.

When conditions became serious and rural people found they could no longer stay where they had been, they began to move about looking for a place where they would be welcome and where they could survive. For many, there was little desire to leave the state, and they attempted to move to

Leaving Muskogee bound for California, 1939. (FSA Collection. Courtesy Library of Congress.)

other places nearby. For example, in 1935 a government official reported trucks moving from the drought stricken area of northwestern Oklahoma to eastern sections of the state where they could at least raise their own food.[8]

Most of those dispossessed from the land seemed to have little direction since the pattern for them was to move aimlessly about the state. Eventually, the trend was for them to gravitate toward the urban areas of the state, especially Oklahoma City. By 1935 a network of "squatter camps" began to emerge around the city.[9] One of the worst of these was the May Avenue Camp where hundreds of indigent families subsisted in unmitigated squalor.

The nature of Oklahoma's agricultural economy, its government, and its social patterns really set the tone for the movement of people. An understanding of transiency and its impact requires a recognition that Oklahoma was a rural state dominated by farm tenancy with an inefficient governmental structure. The conditions of Oklahoma agriculture and the failures of the political system were the major reasons people moved.

Tenancy was an established institution in Oklahoma when the Depression began. In 1930 almost 62 percent of all farmers were tenants[10] and their day to day existence was precarious at best. Studies have shown that even before the thirties transiency was high among tenants. For example, in the twenties at least 43 percent of tenants changed farms each year; in some areas it was as high as 79 percent. As one observer commented, "Oklahoma's tenants were 'like a bunch of rolling stones.' . . . They won't stay put."[11] School statistics reveal the extent of the problem. In districts with large tenant populations, the annual turnover was quite high. As many as one-third of the students, one-half of the faculty, and 40 percent of the administration changed each year.[12] Even before the pressures of the Dust Bowl in the western counties and the depression over all the state became severe, it is quite obvious that Oklahomans were a mobile and migrant people.

When the depression and drought came, the fragile Oklahoma economy and political system collapsed. Technological mechanization on the farms was already twenty years old by the thirties. With the pressures to make the land more productive with as little human labor as possible, and with the technology now available, the stage was set for the scenes painted by Steinbeck where tenants were driven off the land to create larger agricultural units.[13]

Still, it must be remembered that factors other than drought combined to drive the farmers off the land. One student of the period believes that floods were more responsible than dust storms for displacing farmers and notes that 1937 was the year of greatest floods in Oklahoma; it was also the year of greatest exodus. During the flood period, 300,000 migrants arrived in California, many of whom came from Oklahoma.[14]

Non-farm unemployment was also a factor in the increase of transiency. Coal miners in eastern Oklahoma had a high rate of unemployment and many of them were desperate enough to move, especially in 1933.[15] Another factor contributing to transiency but not always recognized as such was the oil boom of the thirties. On the one hand the discovery of oil brought prosperity to some in the midst of depression,

May Avenue Shacktown, Oklahoma City, 1939. (FSA Collection. Courtesy Library of Congress.)

but on the other hand, it contributed to the instability of the population as people moved from place to place to take advantage of the jobs available. The oral history provided by Charlie Stone, a rig builder in Oklahoma, is a poignant example of how lives were disrupted in the search for work.[16]

The Oklahoma economy could not survive such a challenge. One student of the era put it this way: "Serious students must begin with the fact that the 'Okies' could not have stayed on the farms in the Sooner state."[17] Actually, most Oklahoma farmers lived precariously in 1930 when the serious troubles began. Marginal farmers at best, they survived only by moving regularly and living by their wits. Technological mechanization was a major enemy of the tenants. Their farming techniques were outmoded, and their economic base was eroding rapidly. Their education was so poor that adaptation to other occupations was difficult at best. "Even without a Dust Bowl, their situation was desperate."[18] There simply was inadequate opportunity in the Oklahoma economy for much of the state's population.[19]

The weakness of state government in Oklahoma compounded the problem, for neither the governor nor the legislature could provide the leadership needed in this time of severe crisis. State programs for the relief and relocation of displaced persons were insufficient. Even the availability of federal programs from New Deal sources oftentimes created even more suffering. In fact, the policies of the Agricultural Adjustment Act contributed to transiency in Oklahoma. The conservation features of the AAA encouraged taking land out of production and consolidating small farms into larger units.[20] Through both processes the tenant was the loser, and the state government of Oklahoma offered no programs to protect these people. Indeed, Oklahomans forced off the land "appeared as pawns, pushed by powerful masters from Oklahoma into foreign areas where they faced a deadly fate from another set of powerful masters."[21] One student postulates that the real reason for migration was "comprehensive disorganization and incompetence of Oklahoma government at all levels."[22]

Whatever the causes may have been, transiency and migration were major social facts in Oklahoma in the thirties. There is simply no way to estimate the number of Oklahomans who moved during the thirties—either within the state or to other states. By 1938 perhaps as many as one-third of a million people had left the state, but this does not include those who were displaced within Oklahoma. At least 133,000 people left the farm between 1935 and 1940, but

A virtually abandoned street in Caddo, Oklahoma. (FSA Collection. Courtesy Library of Congress.)

there is no systematic way to know where they went.[23]

As is always true of those in the lower economic strata of society, there was disagreement about how badly they suffered and how serious they were about improving their status. For example, the Tulsa *Tribune* deplored the existence of "squatters" on the city's outskirts and believed, "For most of them, this moving from one town to another is one grand vacation, first on one relief agency, then on another."[24]

This viewpoint is hard to contradict, especially when one considers the testimony of those who participated in the exodus. For example, when Studs Terkel interviewed people in the late sixties for his valuable oral history of the depression, he discovered a woman from Oklahoma who had traveled for three years with her husband during the thirties. Her memories of those times were pleasant. She said that it was best for poor people to move about because trouble always seemed to find those who stayed in one place. "It's really a good life, if you're poor and you can manage to move around."[25]

Despite her statement the evidence is persuasive that migration was not voluntary, even in times before the depression. There has always been the element of mobility within American society, and many characterize Americans as a restless people who have always been on the move. This is true, but the transients of the thirties do not necessarily fit that model. For example, in the Dust Bowl section of northwestern Oklahoma, the people were not anxious to pull up their roots and move on. Many of them endured hardship as long as they could. "They were people who had endured hardships as good soldiers in other times of crisis. The thought of leaving hardly occurred to them."[26] Even so, many of them eventually had no choice in the matter. A woman from Eva, Oklahoma, assured a friend in Maryland that the people who were uprooted, however, were not merely drifters as was frequently claimed.[27]

Again, the interpretation of the migrants is contradictory. One authority says that displaced tenants did not seek or find alternative work. Many did not move hoping for improvement; they moved to satisfy their "gypsy desires."[28] But a study of the migrants to California revealed that Oklahomans were transients out of necessity and were hoping to find employment and stability. "From their earliest days in California they embarked upon the struggle for residence."[29] "Little Oklahomas" existed all over California in the thirties, particularly in the Central Valley towns such as Merced, Fresno, and Bakersfield. Even today at least two areas in greater Los Angeles—Garvey Acres and Bell Gardens—still reflect their Oklahoma origins. This might indicate that at least some of the Oklahomans found the permanence they were seeking.[30]

Other evidence, though scanty, exists to support the claim that the movement of Oklahomans was involuntary. Although the spelling and grammar left something to be desired, an unidentified Oklahoman expressed his sentiment in crude verse:[31]

America remember 1928
When to the Poles you go to vote
Hoover's promise true
how he'd put you on your feet,
and he put you on the Soop line too.

A cothouse in Oklahoma City, 1942. (FSA Collection. Courtesy Library of Congress.)

Sold the Old homeplace for Taxes
And in a tent you went to wail
we've got the Hoover Blues

Other Oklahomans expressed much the same sentiment in their poetry:[32]

We have tramped the street enough
Hoover didn't get in his bluff
So Hooverism must die
And we gladly say good-bye.

Although he refers to more than Oklahoma, a resident of Madill revealed something of the involuntary nature of transiency in two lines of a poem:[33]

Ten million people just tramps to roam,
Robbed of their money they have no home.

The impact of transiency can be seen in many ways. For example, the Southern Tenant Farmers Union organized more than eighty local chapters in Oklahoma by 1935, but the migration to California virtually wiped out the movement in the Sooner state.[34] Migrant camps in Oklahoma became sources of diseases, sometimes even of epidemic proportions. Near Oklahoma City a settlement known as the "Kingdom of Junk" was the source of diseases such as typhoid and spinal meningitis, as were similar camps throughout the state. This was also true of those who went to California. Oklahomans in California suffered more from epidemics and deficiency diseases than did local residents and their infant mortality rate was nearly three times the national average.[35]

The treatment of transients has been a matter of controversy for some time. It is well-known that transients were not welcome anywhere in the country. Obviously the transient was either seeking employment or he was a vagrant. In either case he was a threat to the community. In Oklahoma they were not welcome. In 1935 a transient camp on the outskirts of Oklahoma City next to the municipal dump had some 2,000 residents. In order to discourage them the city refused to hire anyone from the camp. In California only one county provided any medical aid to the migrants. Nevertheless, the health of the Oklahomans in California was no worse than that in Oklahoma.[36]

The Oklahomans who moved to California were unique. For one thing, they fiercely maintained their family units at all costs. Certainly, families were shattered, but every effort was made to keep them intact. They moved as much as possible in family groups, perhaps as a holdover from tenant days in Oklahoma when they found their greatest strength in the security of the family. The "Okies" (a term that came to represent the California migrants from Texas and Arkansas as well as Oklahoma) appeared to be unique also in that they often travelled in personal automobiles that usually represented the family's entire net worth. Also they did not readily accept relief. It was considered degrading to be dependent upon someone else; the family should care for its own. Acceptance of relief was an act of desperation.[37]

Those who moved to California were primarily from agricultural backgrounds. In a survey taken in California some 80 percent said that agriculture had been thier sole occupation before migration. Almost no proprietors, managers, or professionals could be found among the migrants,[38] perhaps because they were few in Oklahoma and had a better chance to cope with the depression than those agricultural workers who had no other skills and little education.

Without doubt, transiency had a major impact on Oklahoma in the thirties. Like much of the country, Oklahoma was transformed by the depression and the massive government programs that were created to combat it. Population patterns were changed by drought, floods, farm mechanization, and migration. The state lost a large portion of its population, the majority of which finally found its way to California. California, too, was greatly influenced by the

On the road in Oklahoma. (FSA Collection. Courtesy Library of Congress.)

despised "Okies" (including Texans and Arkansans) and the impact can still be seen in certain sections of the state.

The scars of the depression did not heal easily or rapidly. This was especially true of those who were uprooted and forced into humiliating and degrading roles as the great unwanted mass of humanity. Without doubt, many Oklahomans do not remember those days fondly.

Jobs for Students:

The National Youth Administration in Oklahoma

By Kenneth E. Hendrickson, Jr.

Oklahomans knew economic misery long before 1929. Their suffering merely intensified between that date and the inauguration of Franklin D. Roosevelt in March, 1933. For the farmers one disaster followed another. Wheat fell from $1.05 to $.33 per bushel. Rural property values plummeted and numerous families lost their homes. For many others, even those who retained their land, the outlook was for little more than abject poverty.[1]

Life in the cities was equally miserable for many thousands of people. Relief rolls soared far beyond the capacities of existing agencies to render assistance. In Oklahoma City alone there were more than 7,000 single men unemployed by 1933, and the situation was equally bad in Tulsa and other towns. Particularly hard hit were young people. By 1935 there were 97,000 people between the ages of 16 and 25 in families on relief. Unless they were their family's sole breadwinner, few of them could find jobs. Simultaneously, school enrollments declined. Of 751,842 persons of school age in 1935, only 497,974 were enrolled.

The adult world, confronted with its own problems of employment and survival, gave little attention to the tribulations of youth. The young had little to do but wait, and while they waited they turned to unproductive means of spending the seemingly endless days and weeks and months. Some became wanderers—hoboes—while others turned to crime as they became ever more desperate. The machinery of state government was helpless to assist these people, and even the early New Deal programs rendered aid to only a tiny minority.[2]

That President Roosevelt was sensitive to the problems of youth had already become evident through the creation of the Civilian Conservation Corps in 1933. By 1935 the CCC was well established in Oklahoma, but its advantages were available to only a few young men. There were thousands of others, girls as well as boys, who continued to wait. To meet their needs, at least in part, Roosevelt created the National Youth Administration by Executive Order No. 7086 on June 26, 1935, under authority granted by the Emergency Relief Appropriations Act of April 8. Immediately thereafter, he appointed a National Advisory Committee chaired by Josephine Roche and he named Aubrey Williams to be National Director. At the outset this program met with a generally favorable response, even from the anti-New Deal press. Only the National Education Association voiced strong opposition. Terming it a "raw deal" for the public schools, NEA Executive Secretary Willard E. Givens complained that the NYA would take the control of education away from the states where it belonged. It would also inject politics into education and would be extravagantly expensive.[3]

Designed to provide education, jobs, recreation, counselling, and opportunity for American youth between the ages of 16 and 25, the NYA received its direction and funding from Washington, but it was administered at the state level. The State Youth Director and his staff were responsible ultimately for the implementation of programs, but they were assisted by the public through a State Advisory Committee and Local Advisory Committees at the county and city levels. In Oklahoma the State Advisory Committee was chaired by Governor E. W. Marland who was deeply sympathetic to the NYA and supported it fully. More important, however, were the local committees which were eventually established in most of the counties and towns in the state. The committees, with a membership of six to eight persons, usually public officials, were designed to promote and publicize the NYA, and encourage local groups to co-sponsor work projects. In Oklahoma, as in most other states, this system worked very well and many observers believed that the NYA could not have been effective without it.

Houston Wright, Administrative Assistant to President Henry C. Bennett of Oklahoma A&M, was named Youth Director for Oklahoma. He appointed a staff of five, hired nine clerks and secretaries, and prepared to launch the program with an inaugural budget of $600,000. His first goal was to establish a work program for students still enrolled in school. The task was difficult because the beginning of the academic year was only weeks away and as yet no one knew any of the details. Wright planned eleven district meetings and over 1,000 school administrators attended to receive their orientation. A little later the colleges and universities sent representatives to Oklahoma City for similar purposes and before September 1 a workable plan was adopted for the establishment of work projects and distribution of funds. All the schoolmen of the state, including L. K. Cavelle, Director of the State Department of Vocational Education, pledged support, apparently ignoring the warnings of Willard Givens. However, they recognized that the federal allocation was entirely too small to meet the need and they were uneasy with the fact that many deserving students would probably receive no assistance. They began at once to agitate for more money.[4]

Aubrey Williams and his associates in Washington were anxious to ensure that all official work projects in the schools would be "worthwhile" and they pressured Wright to consider their desires in establishing the program.[5] However, Wright resisted. "We have emphasized quick employment in the school aid program," he wrote, "and as yet have not checked on the type of work performed to see how 'worthwhile' it is." To do so would have been impossible under the circumstances. Too many people needed help urgently for Wright and his staff to worry about the intrinsic value of the tasks performed.[6]

Eventually, most of the school aid projects were designed so that they fell into one of four categories. These were: departmental assistance; construction and maintenance; clerical assistance; and semi-professional assistance. Ninety percent of the jobs fell into one of the first three categories and in spite of efforts to prevent it, the school work program never entirely lost its "makework" reputation. Still, much of the work was useful. At Byng High School in Ada a group of students assisted in the preparation of teaching materials; at El Reno NYA students supervised playground activities at four elementary schools; in Norman they maintained a nursery; at Snyder they carried out a terracing project on nearby farms; at Panola they installed a sewer system in the high school; and in Hobart they operated a cafeteria for underprivileged children. These projects were typical of the hundreds which operated throughout the state from 1935 until 1943, providing part-time employment for as many as 17,000 students per month at an average monthly income of $3.34 and a maximum of $6.00.[7]

The school aid program was popular with those who participated. Schoolmen and students alike were lavish in their praise as reflected in the letters they wrote to administrators in both Oklahoma and Washington. A typical statement was that of Ruth Alexander who wrote to A. H. Parmelee, Principal of Capitol Hill High School in Oklahoma City, as follows:[8]

> During the first semester of this year when I was not working on the N.Y.A., I worked in a private home for my room and board and fifty cents a

> week. This I used for bus fare as we were five miles from school. I also worked in the school cafeteria for my lunch, and the county furnished my books. In order to get pencils, paper, and personal things I sold the lunch that the cafeteria gave me. Hand-me-down clothing was given to me by friends and relatives. Of course, I had to forget all about ball games and school activities, but I'm so determined to finish high school and take nursing that I'd do anything to get that.
>
> During the second semester though (sic) along came the N.Y.A., and I feel all but rich! I eat my lunch now myself, and I've had one pair of silk hose, and I'm going to the Junior Prom! That's all something—believe me. I wish I could let you know just how it feels to be full of food and have real money in your pocket book.

Parmelee, in turn, sent his views to NYA Assistant Director Richard Brown in Washington:[9]

> One hundred ninety-six of our 1400 students are enrolled in NYA and 75% of these earn $6.00 per month. It is extremely satisfying to me to look over this (sic) data and know that a program of this type has helped many boys and girls who otherwise would be deprived of absolute necessities for school attendance. My honest convictions are that the government money alloted (sic) for youth nets more profitable returns than any other government relief expenditure.

In the colleges and universities the NYA program paralleled that in the high schools. The aid recipients, averaging about 5,000 per month, did the same type of work although they received an average of $11.00 per month and a maximum of $15.00. College administrators were also generous with praise. Using adjectives such as "splendid," "wonderful," and "responsible," they were virtually unanimous in their views that the program was useful and should be continued as long as possible. Even more vigorously, they pleaded for greater appropriations so that more young people could receive assistance. The one objection common to almost all school and college administrators was their dread of having to choose recipients from a large and ever-present list of applicants.[10]

Despite the popularity of the school and college aid programs, difficulties concerning the type and quality of the work and the inadequacy of allocations persisted. Ultimately, these problems led to the creation of the High School and College Work Councils in 1941. The High School Council, made up of seven principals and superintendents, was chaired by Eli C. Foster, Principal of Central High School in Tulsa. Foster and his colleagues sent investigators into the field in the spring of 1941 where they visited 332 schools and conducted thirty conferences. Their reports showed that the NYA was still extremely popular; indeed most schools had long waiting lists, but there remained many weaknesses. Principals often treated the program in cursory fashion, failing to give adequate time and attention to such vital activities as selection; and work assignments rarely coincided with the students' interests or aptitudes. On the other hand, many administrators seemed genuinely interested in improvement and participated with apparent eagerness in the numerous conferences.

By the end of May, 1941, the Council had reached several conclusions upon which to base their recommendations. These suggested that the effectiveness of the program was directly related to the efforts of the principals and their supervising teachers in each school. They should conduct the program so as to produce results of lasting value and at the same time train young people in some useful skill. These were laudable goals, but of course they differed very little from the original mandate of Aubrey Williams that school work projects should be "worthwhile," and it is highly debatable that they were ever attained.

The College Work Council was chaired by President M. L. Wardell of Oklahoma University. Formed later in 1941, it operated through a series of conferences designed to produce more effective coordination of the college program, more careful selection and monitoring of projects, and greater regard for the welfare of the students. As in the case of the School Work Councils, there is no way to measure the effectiveness of this effort.[11]

NYA workers on the O.U. campus in Norman. (Courtesy Western History Collections, University of Oklahoma Library.)

Popular though it was, the school work phase of the NYA was neither as elaborate nor as significant as the out-of-school work project, for, although the latter served fewer people, it accomplished more useful results and led directly to the important defense training projects which developed during the last days of the NYA.

The out-of-school work program began in the spring of 1936 with the opening of Camp Parthenia for girls. A second camp began operations at Stillwater in January, 1937, and a third opened at Cordell in February. The major purpose of these camps was to rehabilitate the health and morale of the young women who attended. Little was done at first to provide them with vocational training. By 1938, however, a resident center vocational training program had grown out of the girls' camp experiment and functioned effectively until 1943. Meanwhile, the girls' camps were successful in achieving their limited objectives. Those who attended learned how to eat properly, to care for their bodies; to have motivation and self-esteem. While attending a conference of NYA Directors at Hyde Park in 1937, Houston Wright told President Roosevelt that the 500 enrollees at the Stillwater camp had gained an average of ten pounds apiece. Roosevelt complimented Wright for adding two and one-half tons of beef to the youth of Oklahoma, but he did not provide funding for the continuation of the girls' camp program.[12]

By the mid-thirties the need for NYA participation was particularly acute in the western counties, yet the population was sparse and did not lend itself to normal program operations. Thus it was recognized that resident centers were needed in order to provide NYA opportunities for youth from these areas where it was difficult to develop permanent out-of-school work programs. The centers were open to any youth qualified for NYA, however, and before the end of the thirties Oklahoma had twenty of them with a total capacity of 2,885 and ranging in size from 50 to 475.

A typical Resident Center project was that located on the 101 Ranch near Ponca City, home of Governor Marland. The center was established in 1938 when the Farm Security Administration conveyed a portion of the old 101 Ranch to the NYA, along with fifty buildings, all in a state of disrepair. Fifty boys were brought to the site where they replaced or remodelled all of the buildings and created a dormitory, a recreation center, barns, a small slaughterhouse, wood and metal working shops, a foundry, a blacksmith shop, and an auto repair shop. After settling in they began raising cattle, pigs, and chickens.[13]

Buildings on the 101 Ranch used for the NYA Project. (Courtesy Western History Collections, University of Oklahoma Library.)

In addition to the 101 Ranch project there were five major boys' centers located at Miami, Jay, Chickasha, Lawton, and Tonkawa. The latter, a radio training center established in 1940, was the largest in the state with a capacity of 475 youth. The residents there studied mathematics, science, blueprint reading, and other subjects related to radio operation. They learned about the construction of transmitters, receivers, public address systems, interoffice communications systems, and radio testing equipment; they also built radio components which were used by municipal, state, and federal agencies all over the state. At other boys' centers the residents were trained in woodworking, electricity, auto mechanics, blacksmithing, welding, and farming.

The major girls' resident centers were located at Shawnee, Hobart, Altus, and Weatherford. There the young women learned office skills, sewing, arts, crafts, and homemaking.

Like the boys, they also received instruction in self-improvement and counselling. Some young women also attended coeducational resident centers. These were located at Stillwater, Langston, Alva, and Miami, all on college campuses. The residents took regular college courses in addition to special training in pottery, farming, wood and metal working, cosmetology, and sewing. All the residents received a stipend of $30 per month from which the NYA deducted sufficient sums to pay for their room and board.[14]

Not all the out-of-school work projects were conducted at resident centers; in fact most were not. NYA projects and workshops were to be found in communities all over the state. These evolved from an early phase which concentrated on park and school beautification, through a second phase during which most of the work was on construction projects, into a final period when almost all projects

Renovating a building on 101 Ranch for the NYA Project. (Courtesy Western History Collections, University of Oklahoma Library.)

emphasized national defense training in a workshop setting.

The school beautification program was important in the beginning because it enabled young people living in sparsely populated areas to participate in NYA before the inauguration of the resident center program. Moreover, it benefited numerous communities. Under the program NYA workers set out hundreds of trees, planted countless shrubs and flowers, resodded school grounds, built retaining walls and fences, and repaired and painted a large number of buildings.

The construction program emphasized road repair at first, but soon broadened to include the building of non-resident youth centers and workshops. The structures were put up by NYA workers, then equipped and used by out-of-school youth whether enrolled in NYA or not. Typical of these centers was the one at Okmulgee where four buildings were constructed on a twelve-acre plot near the city. In this complex the NYA youth received vocational training for the trades and industries. They built tables and chairs and other articles of furniture, and they also received instruction in homemaking, sewing, cooking, marketing, budgeting, and the care of children. Another typical project was at El Reno where the NYA purchased a six-room house and remodeled it into an office and youth center. From this center NYA workers were dispatched about the city to carry out numerous projects. One group supervised playground activities in the public schools. Another built playground equipment for the municipal parks and schools, and yet another led nature study groups on outings.[15]

To accompany the work projects, of whatever type, Houston Wright and his colleagues developed a related training, guidance, and counselling program of significant proportions. This program was designed to promote concern for health and hygiene, to provide vocational guidance and counselling for youth still in school, and finally, to provide vocational guidance and counselling for those who were out of school.

A NYA Music Project for blind youth at O.U. (Courtesy Western History Collections, University of Oklahoma Library.)

The in-school phase of the program was carried out in cooperation with school officials who were provided with workbooks containing a full course in personal improvement which they were asked to conduct for all NYA students. The course revolved around the identification of abilities and interests, feasible vocational alternatives, and the process of bringing these together. It was carried out through a series of conferences held after school hours and was conducted by guidance counsellors or designated teachers. Its success is almost impossible to measure statistically, but without doubt it was useful to at least some of the participants. In any event, it was popular. Within a few weeks of its inauguration in the spring of 1936 it was operating in more than 300 schools.[16]

The guidance and counselling program for out-of-school youth was not particularly effective, at least during its first three or four years. One major problem was the enormous range of intelligence and background among the out-of-school youth which made it difficult to apply any standard approach when dealing with them. Another was the fact that counselling was provided by project supervisors, who had insufficient time to do it properly on a largely hit-or-miss basis. In this process there were some efforts to place young people in permanent jobs through cooperation with the State Employment Service, but this too met with only marginal success, at least during the early years. Gradually, the OSES assumed greater control over the process of placement and achieved better results, but it was not until the war that NYA became a virtual feeder of young labor to industry.[17]

The Oklahoma NYA began to operate health clinics in conjunction with the guidance program in 1936. These clinics provided examination, counselling, and instruction in first aid, hygiene, and accident prevention. All were both popular and useful. However, they were not continued because of inadequate funding. Later, in 1940, the national administration required the establishment of health programs in all the states and provided money for support. This program remained in effect until the NYA was terminated in 1943 and was very important because it was necessary to certify that young workers hired by defense industries in cities all over the country were in good health.[18]

During its first five years of operation in Oklahoma the NYA was reasonably successful. In spite of the problems which inevitably developed in the administration of such a complex program, most observers gave the program very high marks. There were, however, certain facets of the program which were far below par, and among these the most prominent was the treatment of blacks. They did not receive anything even approximating a fair share of the resources allocated to the Sooner State. Even though the national administration prohibited discrimination, the NYA Negroes in Oklahoma were segregated and provided with only an absolute minimum of assistance. Moreover, Wright appointed only three black members to a staff which eventually totaled 125, so even those black youth who were fortunate enough to receive assistance almost inevitably found themselves under white supervision.

Oklahoma had a Negro State Advisory Committee chaired by President J. W. Sanford of Langston and including Roscoe Dunjee, editor of the Oklahoma City *Black Dispatch*, and Sam Sadler, Principal of Manual Training High School in Muskogee.[19] Although there is little evidence of their activities available, this group appears to have been relatively accommodating and willing to accept a segregated program. However, not all black leaders were so pliable. The first State Director of Negro Affairs was Lawrence Burr who served from 1935 to 1937. Burr was considerably rankled by the fact that he received an annual salary of $1,600 as compared to $4,500 for Wright. Moreover, Burr had no office space and no staff. He attempted to buck the tide of obstructionism until the spring of 1937, but achieved very meager results. By that time there was only one Negro Resident Center, located at Langston University, and a grand total of only 729 black youth per month were receiving NYA aid throughout the state. All the supervisors on black projects were white.

Having become thoroughly disgusted by April, 1937, Lawrence Burr attempted to confront the race issue in Oklahoma when he wrote to Mary McLeod Bethune, National Director of Negro Affairs, to complain about the unsatisfactory conditions he had witnessed for two years. He invited her to come to Oklahoma and "see it in the raw," hoping she would be jolted sufficiently to demand change. However, he could have saved himself the trouble. Upon receiving his letter, Mrs. Bethune simply turned it over to Assistant Director Richard Brown who relayed it to Houston Wright along with a suggestion that Burr be fired for "disloyalty."[20]

Anne L. Caution succeeded Burr as Director of Negro Affairs a little later in 1937. She was prepared to accept segregation and to help train young blacks to do "Negro Work." She wrote, "They must learn to do well the things they will have to do."[21]

From 1937 to 1939 the Negro program improved considerably if measured in terms of participation. Resident Centers were opened in Oklahoma City, Tulsa, Chickasha, Guthrie, and Valiant; and two more were planned for Ardmore and Watonga. There was also a non-resident shop project in Muskogee. In these projects the girls learned homemaking and sewing and the boys received instruction in woodwork, metalwork, nursery work, and soil conservation. By December, 1939, there were 416 black youth employed out of school and 91 in Resident Centers. The number receiving in-school aid is unknown, but was probably somewhat in excess of 2,000.[22]

Measured in terms of quality the black program showed little improvement by the end of 1939. There were still no black supervisors, facilities and equipment were shoddy, and there were occasional reports of mistreatment. In some cities such as Watonga and Ardmore, there was open resistance to the Negro program on the part of city officials. On the other hand, there were a few bright spots in an otherwise dreary panorama of segregation and discrimination. One of these was the girls' workshop in Chickasha. Here nineteen girls began patching quilts in 1937. They met in one room of a dilapidated building equipped with two benches and a pot-bellied stove. They came from homes of utter squalor and most of them were filthy, dejected, and withdrawn. To assist these girls Anne L. Caution persuaded a certain Miss Effie Bullock to assume supervisory duties. Whether Miss Bullock was white or black is unknown, but in any event she threw herself into her work with great enthusiasm, although without pay. (After awhile Miss Bullock was given a salary of $40 per month.) She taught the girls personal hygiene and sewing skills and gradually they began to exhibit small sparks of interest, perhaps even hope for the future. They converted their workroom into a bright, clean, almost cheerful place and they began to make dresses and to repair furniture. Their efforts attracted the attention of city officials who purchased and donated a large seven-room house to the project so that it could be made a resident center.

The girls in the Chickasha Project carried their training back to their homes. They made wearing apparel for other members of their families and some of them painted and redecorated their houses. They also formed a choral group which eventually received state-wide recognition. But for all of that the Chickasha Project was small and unusual, if not unique. In general, the Negro NYA program in Oklahoma remained a dismal failure until the end.[23]

Press coverage of the NYA was almost unanimously positive during the peacetime phase of operations from 1935 until 1941. Typical of the coverage was an editorial in the Madill *Record* on February 15, 1937, which declared:[24]

> There have been criticisms of all other phases of government work but no word against the NYA. Citizens in general are for the movement realizing it helps the youth of the state.

On March 25, 1937, the Watonga *Republican* published a special section on the NYA which included numerous photographs of local projects and this highly complimentary evaluation:[25]

> An infant wandering around in swaddling clothes a few months ago, the NYA has grown to mansized proportions and in Oklahoma today it can be said perhaps that no single educational program has been introduced within the last decade that compares in scope to that of the NYA.

Yet another example is that of the Pauls Valley *Daily Democrat* which on May 2, 1938, featured a front page story on the forthcoming dedication of an NYA building in the town. The story included a graphic description of the construction of the building and its uses and revealed that Mayor Mason Hart had proclaimed a two-hour holiday to begin at noon on May third so that everyone could attend the dedication and partake of the giant barbecue feast which was planned.[26]

One major exception to the otherwise favorable attitude of the press was the *Daily Oklahoman* which was lukewarm at best, and occasionally hostile. One instance of hostility occurred on August 8, 1936, when the paper reported that Houston Wright had received a pay raise in such a way as to suggest that Wright was a boondoggler.[27] The article was regarded as a matter so serious that Assistant Director Richard Brown in Washington asked Congressman Jed Johnson for advice. Johnson suggested that the matter should be ignored since he believed that the *Daily Oklahoman* was only looking for ways to embarrass the NYA. The paper should be given no opportunity to raise critical issues, especially where money was concerned.[28]

The beginning of World War II marked the opening of a new and final era in the history of the NYA in Oklahoma. As war clouds formed over Europe, rain clouds formed over the Sooner State. In the western counties the Dust Bowl conditions began to ease. Agricultural conditions also improved somewhat in eastern counties and as a result work was more plentiful than it had been in years. In the fall of 1940 the draft began and young men were pulled into the armed forces. Many volunteered before they could be called. All these developments reduced the pool of youth eligible for NYA.

In response to new conditions the ideals and purposes of the NYA began to change. For some time Director Aubrey Williams and his associates in Washington had ceased to think of the program as a temporary relief measure and had begun to think of it as a permanent feature of American life. They were prepared to adapt to current needs. If fewer youth were available for the program, they were prepared to recruit. If the nation required an increasing number of individuals trained in defense-related skills, the NYA would assist in providing them. Relief would be minimized or eliminated as a primary reason for the existence of the program, and other needs would replace it. Thus it was decided that certain skills such as woodworking, sewing, sheetmetal work, welding, radio and automotive repair, and foundry work were vital to the needs of national defense. The NYA now allocated more of its financial resources to the purchase of training equipment and the hiring of skilled supervisors and reduced allocations to the in-school work program. Now the agency shifted rapidly from one devoted to relief to one devoted primarily to highly technical work training. This shift was met by cries of opposition from the professional educators who regarded it as a major threat.[29]

When the defense training program began Aubrey Williams and John W. Studebaker, Director of the United States Office of Education, agreed that the classroom portions of the training would be under the USOE and the work portions under NYA, but this did not satisfy some educators who charged that "productive work" was actually "shop training" of an inferior sort. They insisted that public vocational schools could do the job better and cheaper and their charges produced tension which severely weakened the claims of the NYA that their contribution to the defense effort was critical.[30]

With tension and uncertainty fostering ever bolder opposition, the fight in Congress to preserve the NYA during 1941-42 fiscal year was bitter and prolonged. The opponents included not only those who professed to fear the spectre of federal intervention into the field of vocational education, but also those who were generally hostile to the New Deal. Favoring the NYA were many of the manufacturers who employed NYA-trained people in their shops, those who believed the relief program still had something to offer people in their areas, and progressive educators and others who desired to see the NYA become a permanent agency.[31]

Public Law 146 which resulted from the great debate in 1941 authorized the NYA to carry on a program of "construction, production, professional and clerical projects, and resident centers; and a youth work defense program to furnish work experience preparatory to employment in a defense industry." In Oklahoma the program, now headed by Bruce Carter who succeeded Wright in March, 1940, rapidly shifted in this direction with defense training centers set up in Chickasha, Enid, Mangum, Oklahoma City, Tulsa, Muskogee, Ardmore, Okmulgee, Shawnee, and Durant. By the spring of 1942 there were approximately 3,500 trainees located in these centers.[32]

After another furious debate in the spring of 1942, Congress voted to continue the NYA for yet another year. Now, however, the program was to be devoted entirely to training and production for the war effort. Need was entirely eliminated as a requirement for eligibility. The administration was also modified substantially in September, 1942, when control of the NYA was transfered to the War Manpower Commission. Thus, the agency lost its independence. State administrations were abolished and the program was operated henceforward through a series of regional offices. Oklahoma was in Region IX along with Arkansas, Missouri, and Kansas.[33]

Within each state, administration of the program was further streamlined with the creation of War Production Training Centers, or "Master Projects." There were eight of these centers in Oklahoma located at Tonkawa, Oklahoma City, Tulsa, Durant, Cordell, Shawnee, Chickasha, and Muskogee, with subsidiary units in seventeen other cities. Some of these centers were former resident centers or non-resident workshops and some were not, but in any case they were established with modern equipment (whenever possible), and professional supervisors. They provided training in sheetmetal work, welding, radio repair, auto mechanics, woodwork, and sewing. During their one year of operation they trained nearly 20,000 workers and assigned them to jobs in private industry all over the country.[34]

Although there was opposition to the Defense Training Program in rural states like Oklahoma on grounds that it drew young people away from the farm and thus hampered

The NYA National Office countered immediately with a refutation of Givens's charges showing that he misused the figures in arriving at his cost estimate—that in fact the

Governor Leon C. "Red" Phillips. (Courtesy Western History Collections, University of Oklahoma Library.)

maximum cost would be approximately $725 per trainee per year by 1944. Their refutation also showed that the NYA did not duplicate the vocational school programs, but in fact added two dimensions to technical training which could not be provided by the public schools. Those dimensions were speed and flexibility. The NYA was equipped to take unskilled persons and train them sufficiently in six to eight weeks to operate a single machine and thus to perform useful work. The NYA was further equipped to assign such people to work locations anywhere in the country at times when they were most needed. The public vocational schools could perform neither of these functions.[39]

These were powerful arguments, but there is no way to determine the extent of their effect on public opinion. The McKellar Bill never became law, but on the other hand the Byrd Committee eventually recommended liquidation and supporters of the NYA did not fare well in the congressional floor debates which occurred early in the summer of 1943 after the conclusion of the Byrd Committee's proceedings. Those who wanted liquidation argued that the New Deal relief programs had served their purpose and were now an expensive luxury. The defense training aspect of the program, they argued, lacked significant value, and the educational aspect could easily be replaced by state-financed vocational education programs. Indeed, many congressmen professed to fear that continuation of the NYA carried with it the danger of ever greater federal control of education in general even though there is little evidence to suggest that similar fears existed at the state level.

Two Oklahoma congressmen, A. S. "Mike" Monroney and Jed Johnson, spoke in the debate. Monroney joined with the opposition to the NYA saying that although he had supported the agency in 1942, he had now changed his mind. He was convinced that the NYA had outlived its usefulness and had become a drag on rural labor in Oklahoma.

Congressman Jed Johnson. (Courtesy Western History Collections, University of Oklahoma Library.)

He also professed to agree with those who called the NYA an unnecessary competition with public education and a burdensome expense.

Congressman Johnson allied himself with those who defended the NYA record, attempted to demonstrate its usefulness to the war effort, and pointed to the possibility of a

orientation. The BM&E, on the other hand, owned a line which ran parallel with the long axis of the Panhandle. All had approximately the same service mileage and all were heavily dependent on agricultural produce for local traffic.

Wheat was the Panhandle's pre-eminent crop. Although the total number of farms there decreased each decade after 1910, the production of wheat increased, depending, of course, on the capricious whims of the weather. Farmers in the area learned to carry the surpluses of fat years over to the lean ones. One longtime resident recalled that the accepted yardstick for agricultural success was:

> One crop in three years—people can get along
> One crop in two years—prosperity
> One crop per year—Boom!

By the late twenties, 64 percent of the farmers in the heart of the southern Great Plains were dependent on cash crops—usually wheat—for a living. Oklahoma's Cimarron County reflected this. Its farmers produced only 590,000 bushels of wheat in 1924, but four seasons later their production had risen to nearly 2.5 million bushels. Then came what one writer has called the "super-duper, ultra-terrific wheat year"—1931. The total wheat production for Cimarron County alone was nearly 6 million bushels in 1931. Unfortunately, it was a mixed blessing. On June 10, 1931, number one wheat at Amarillo brought fifty cents per bushel, but as the bounteous harvest reached the elevators prices plummeted. Wheat sold for only twenty-four cents per bushel at Keyes later that summer, and bankruptcy resulted for numerous farmers.[2]

The Missouri-Kansas-Texas Railroad (M-K-T or Katy), which acceded to the properties of the Beaver Road on July 1, 1931, expected that at least 6,000 cars of wheat would be originated on the BM&E as a result of 1931's bumper crop. By early July, 3,000 loads had been billed on the BM&E and the M-K-T in western Oklahoma. Nevertheless, those farmers who could do so were holding their wheat; Katy officials estimated that 60 percent of the harvest would be stored for future shipment.[3]

When Katy assumed operations of the Beaver Road, ninety-six unbilled and unsold cars of wheat—loaded at Mouser and Hough—plugged the Hooker yards. With the price of wheat depressed and their bins filled to capacity, elevator operators had loaded these box cars subject to billing on consignment. They were eventually moved to Hutchinson, Kansas, Houston, Texas, or other points while the consignees hoped for a rise in prices on the grain market. The contents of these cars finally were sold en-route, although the process was time consuming and wasteful of ton miles. In August, farmers received a paltry twenty cents per bushel at Amarillo. After fifteen months, and another growing season, Hooker elevators were paying only twenty-six cents per bushel. The full force of the depression had come to the Panhandle.[4]

Nature then attempted a total eclipse of the region. As early as 1895, the *Alva Review* took note of a severe dust storm which whirled into the area from the north. Another preview of the Dirty Thirties occurred in the Panhandle during March of 1923 when a devastating wind swept in from the north and west. "We do not think the scene will be witnessed again for generations to come," opined the optimistic editor of the *Hooker Advance*. "Blissful peace and happiness," he continued, "is always found on the prairies, where man finds contentment and prosperity." His prophecy was sadly in error. In 1932 the winds were strong—strong enough on April 17 to blow down the BM&E's engine house at Beaver. The following year was hot, dry, and windy. The wheat harvest for the three-county Oklahoma Panhandle averaged only 18/100 of a bushel per acre, and near Hooker some sixty cattle per day died of a disease brought on by the dust storms. An April storm in 1934 dumped dirt from the Panhandle on the Capitol in Washington, D.C. Yet there was enough rain that season to produce a 3.5 million bushel wheat crop.[5]

into her home. Men frequently grew beards. One explained, wryly: "Whiskers are necessary these days to prevent facial erosion."[8]

The combination of economic depression and Dust Bowl conditions drove people from the land without mercy. In one Texas County township along the BM&E, only eight places out of a possible 136 were still occupied by those who had made the original homestead entry. Early in March, 1936, a newspaper in that county carried two notices of foreclosure proceedings and nine notices of sheriff's sales. Although leaving the homeland was a tragic experience, remaining, too, was a grim business. A veteran section foreman who stayed through those dark days later said, "We lived through it, but I don't know how."[9]

With no grass and only a few weeds on his 640 acres, a farmer near Eva decided in May, 1935, to ship his few remaining cattle to more fertile pastures in the central part of Oklahoma. His twenty-seven head, comprising a partial load, were billed on the BM&E for $46. The same animals were returned to him in the fall on a special 85 percent drought rate. A weary but helpful train crew unloaded them in the dead of the night, and an even wearier owner drove them home at dawn.[10]

Meanwhile, the wheels of government finally ground out some assistance. A thoughtful contemporary observer commented that "the benefit payments under the AAA and the wage payments from the Federal work projects were all that have saved a large territory in the Panhandle from abandonment. Another government project fostered the development of shelter belts.[11]

During 1936, a total of forty-five dust storms roared across the Panhandle. Prospects for recovery looked bleak, and one group of experts recommended that the government purchase and permanently retire 2.25 million acres of land in the affected area. Later in the year, President Franklin D. Roosevelt received a report which chronicled the origins of the Dust Bowl conditions. In summary, government researchers determined that:

A) Too much marginal land had been plowed up
B) The grasslands had been overstocked
C) Cash crop farming had disastrously led to a lack of crop rotation and to an overdependence on wheat
D) Farmers had engaged in improper methods and techniques of farming, land management, and water conservation.

Even as the New Deal attempted to ameliorate these problems, weather conditions worsened in 1937. Storms began as early as January, continued in February, and intensified in March. On March 21, schools in the Panhandle and those as far east as Woodward were forced to close due to a severe dust storm. Before the year ended no less than 110 "destructive duststorms" raked the Panhandle. Cimarron County experienced crop failures in 1937 and 1938, although Beaver and Texas counties each had partial crops both years. Over seventy storms hit Cimarron, Texas, and Beaver counties in 1939; fewer than before, yet the dirt blizzard of March 11 was proclaimed the worst of all.[12]

Duststorm, Keyes, Oklahoma, 1937. (Courtesy of Donovan L. Hofsommer.)

gave chase in a Model A Ford. Parks had earlier placed a twelve-mile-per-hour slow order on a stretch of track near Muncy but as the cars hit the down hill grade toward Goff Creek they safely passed over the "slow" track at more than fifty miles per hour. Meanwhile, a thoroughly alarmed W. C. Anderson, the agent at Eva, warned the Hooker office that he had just seen boxcars flying by his bay window. The agent at Hooker, E. B. Parks, passed the message to section foreman J. R. Rone, who promptly removed a rail at the west end of the Hooker yard. Fortunately, a forced derailment was unnecessary. The itinerant cars negotiated the bridges over Goff Creek but slowed on the uphill grade near Hovey. By this time Parks and the elevator man had caught up with them. They boarded the cars and set the brakes lest they continue their unauthorized journey. Not surprisingly, the dispatcher subsequently issued an order that brakes be set thereafter on all cars at sidings along the BM&E.[15]

Throughout the 1930s crews were admonished by dispatchers on all Panhandle roads to operate their trains "under full control" and to "look out for sand on track," particularly at locations known for their troublesome

A dust-clogged cut, 1937. (Byron Bates Collection, courtesy of Donovan L. Hofsommer.)

nature. These were duly enumerated in orders for each train and, on the Rock Island at least, dispatchers, who had been fooled before, frequently added: ". . . and at all other points liable to be affected."[16]

It was much the same on the Beaver Road where standing orders reminded engine crews that they should "expect to find sand over the rails between milepost 73 and 77." This four-mile stretch was always troublesome, but farther west, at milepost 103 the cuts became so thoroughly filled with dirt in 1937 that two steam shovels were dispatched to clear them. Operated by what BM&E crews called "Dinky Skinners," these Katy employees and their steam shovels spent several days opening the road. Meanwhile, service to Keyes was indefinitely suspended. Elsewhere, many shallow cuts simply disappeared when the track was jacked up to rest on the dirt ballast recently deposited there by a passing storm.[17]

Opening the Beaver Road near Keyes, Oklahoma, 1937. (Byron Bates Collection, courtesy of Donovan L. Hofsommer.)

Railroad companies and their employees had suffered collectively with Panhandle shippers and the general public during the Great Depression. Many laborers were furloughed and one railroad, the Rock Island, went bankrupt while the Katy, BM&E's parent, should have. Only the Santa Fe, with a stronger financial base, enjoyed relative stability. All Panhandle carriers pared service and deferred maintenance but none abandoned lines in the area. Yet the fact that they survived at all seemed to give them strength. Similarly, survival brought pride for those who chose to remain on the land. Now they would resolutely address the need to produce agricultural commodities for the war effort. It was the same for the railroads and their employees. They faced the prospect of prosperity and the burdens of World War II traffic with a confidence and determination born of grim days now past.

Oklahoma Indian Reform in Crisis:

John Collier & the Thomas-Rogers Act

By Kenneth R. Philp

On March 23, 1934, John Collier, the new commissioner of Indian Affairs under President Franklin D. Roosevelt, met with more than 2,000 members of the Five Civilized Tribes at Muskogee, Oklahoma.[1] Collier told the Indians that:[2]

> There is a tide in the affairs of man,
> Which, taken at the flood leads on to fortune,
> Omitted, all the voyage of their life
> Is bound in shallows and miseries.

The commissioner cited these lines from William Shakespeare to gain support for the Wheeler-Howard bill which proposed to reverse the federal Indian policy of land allotment.

Collier had travelled to Muskogee because he wanted to stop the alienation of Indian land and the suppression of tribal institutions that had occurred after the passage of the

On March 20, 1934, Collier met with the Comanches, Kiowas, and the representatives of fourteen smaller tribes at the Anadarko High School. The commissioner stressed that the Indians had good reasons to be suspicious because in the past they had been misled by the government concerning the benefits of land allotment. According to Collier, the Comanche, Kiowa, Wichita, and Apache Reservation originally had 2,500,000 acres but only 596,000 acres remained under Indian title. The commissioner admitted that many individuals had successfully held on to their allotments, but this did not help the 3,742 persons born since the passage of the Dawes Act.[8]

After Collier finished his presentation, Indian spokesmen asked numerous questions about whether they would lose their property rights if they formed a colony or reservation and turned their allotments over to community control. Morris Bedoka, a delegate for the Caddo-Delaware-Wichita Indians, wondered if they would retain subsurface rights to their allotments and receive reimbursement if they eventually left the reservation. Collier indicated that reimbursement was not required and he promised to amend the Wheeler-Howard bill to protect individual ownership of oil and other subsurface minerals.[9]

Jasper Saunkeah, a Kiowa, then asked if the bill forced individuals who owned allotments to give their property to undeserving landless Indians. Collier replied that certificates issued by the government would guarantee the right to use their allotments but heirship land would be purchased for distribution to needy tribesmen. Ernest Thompson, a Kaw, noted that similar promises had been made in treaties but they were usually broken. He argued that the bill would promote segregation and isolate the Indians from their white neighbors.[10]

Before the Anadarko Congress ended, almost all of the tribes who lived in western Oklahoma expressed their desire to continue under the allotment system. The Arapaho, Comanche, Kaw, Pawnee, Ponca, Otoe, and Tonkawa Indians all submitted resolutions against the Wheeler-Howard bill. Other tribes such as the Cheyenne, Sac and Fox, and Absentee Shawnee wanted more time to study the measure before making up their minds.[11]

On March 22 and 23, Collier met with representatives of the Five Civilized Tribes at the Muskogee City Hall and Federal Courtroom. Many of the Indians at this meeting opposed Collier for religious reasons. They listened to advice from G. E. E. Lindquist, a former member of the Board of Indian Commissioners and a missionary from Lawrence, Kansas. Lindquist had preceded Collier throughout Oklahoma and organized missionaries and Christian Indians against the Wheeler-Howard bill because it supposedly fostered paganism.[12] Lindquist issued a press release which claimed that Collier's proposal was "socialism and communism in the rankest sense."[13]

The delegates at Muskogee also were influenced by Joseph Bruner, a sixty-two year old full blood Creek from Sapulpa, Oklahoma. An apostle of assimilation, Bruner was an oil, real estate, and insurance businessman. Shortly after Collier's appointment as commissioner in April 1933, Bruner helped organize the National Indian Confederacy and became its elected chief. The members of this pan-Indian organization included prominent attorneys, businessmen, and politicians who belonged to the Five Civilized Tribes. Bruner had invited Collier to attend an NIC meeting at Wewoka to discuss the formulation of an Indian program. When Collier refused this request and drew up the Wheeler-Howard bill without Indian input, Bruner decided to oppose the government.[14]

In his opening remarks at the Muskogee Congress, Collier tried to dispel rumors fostered by Bruner and Lindquist at the Wheeler-Howard bill was synonymous with communism, socialism, and paganism. Collier indicated that his plans for setting up Indian colonies or reservations would hardly apply to eastern Oklahoma because land allotments there were too widely scattered for consolidation. These reassurances did not prevent the Indians from asking pointed questions. They wanted to know if the bill

Senator Elmer Thomas, of Oklahoma, had excluded the Indians of his state from important sections of the IRA because he concluded that they applied only to tribes in the far Southwest. These sections extended restrictions on Indian land, permitted the creation of new reservations, and provided for limited self-government in order to secure money from the $10 million credit fund. Thomas did allow Oklahoma Indians to come under sections of the IRA that ended land allotment and restored surplus land.[19] This enabled the Kiowa, Comanche, and Apache Indians to gain control over 600 acres of abandoned townsite land which was valued for possible oil exploration.[20] The IRA also provided $250,000 for tuition and scholarships to Indian students, gave Indians preference for positions in the Indian Bureau, and authorized an annual appropriation of $2 million for the purchase of land for landless Indians.[21]

Because he had been unable to consult with the Indians of Oklahoma during the closing days of Congress, Thomas asked Collier to accompany him on a trip to learn about their reaction to the passage of the Indian Reorganization Act. This second series of Indian Congresses met at Muskogee, Miami, Pawhuska, Pawnee, Shawnee, Concho, and Anadarko during October, 1934. Most of the Indians who attended these meetings, with the exception of many full blood members of the Five Civilized Tribes, were pleased that Thomas had excluded them from the provisions of the IRA that permitted the creation of new reservations administered by tribal governments. Nevertheless, many delegates wanted restrictions on their land allotments extended and the right to incorporate tribal business committees so they could secure loans from the IRA's revolving credit fund.[22]

After these congresses ended, Thomas consulted with Collier and Will Rogers, the chairman of the House Indian Affairs Committee. They drafted the Thomas-Rogers bill to meet the special needs of Oklahoma Indians. This measure extended restrictions on land owned by individuals with one-half or more Indian blood. It permitted the Secretary of

Senator Elmer Thomas. (Courtesy Western History Collection, University of Oklahoma Library.)

the Interior to remove restrictions on Indians with less than one-half blood after he consulted with a competency commission that would meet once every four years. The Secretary of the Interior also had jurisdiction over the estates of deceased members of the Osage and Five Civilized Tribes with more than one-half blood. Moreover, Oklahoma courts could not appoint guardians for full bloods without the Secretary's approval.[23]

The Thomas-Rogers bill provided for tribal self-government, credit, and additional money for Indian educational and health care facilities. Groups of Indians who agreed to live on tribal property purchased under the IRA's land

Angie Debo, a noted Oklahoma historian, has pointed out that the Oklahoma Indian Welfare Act led to renewed interest in tribal affairs among the Five Civilized Tribes. But these Indians refused to draft constitutions and charters of incorporation. They continued to operate under 1906 congressional legislation which provided for chiefs or governors appointed by the President. Formal self-government was rejected by the Five Civilized Tribes because over 50 percent of their population consisted of assimilated mixed-bloods who lived on widely scattered land allotments or in towns in different parts of Oklahoma. They also lacked the necessary tribal land for successful self-goverment. Except for the Chickasaws and Choctaws, who owned coal and asphalt deposits, only a few hundred acres remained under tribal control.[34]

Several groups of landless full blood members of the Five Civilized Tribes did relocate on property acquired under the IRA's land purchase program. They established subsistence homestead communities but this experiment in communal living was not very successful. The Creeks at the towns of Alabama-Quassarte, Kialigee, and Thlopthlocco, discovered that their new property was subject to flooding. The United Cherokee Keetoowah Band near Proctor voluntarily placed their small number of allotments under tribal control but the government failed to purchase the necessary additional land required for a viable economic community.[35] Fifty-seven Cherokee families settled on 1,489 acres at Wilburton and McCurtain. These Indians planted gardens and built homes with relief money from the Resettlement Administration, but they found it difficult to develop a viable tribal economy on submarginal land.[36]

The Oklahoma Welfare Act authorized loans to individual Indians from a special $2 million credit fund to help combat the depression. By 1942, 395 members of the Cheyenne and Arapaho, Kiowa, Pawnee, Quapaw, and Shawnee tribes had received loan commitments totalling $286,000.[37] A high delinquency rate of almost 6 percent occurred because the money was used to improve small unproductive parcels of land. This problem was especially troublesome at the Colony Rehabilitation Project in western Oklahoma where the Cheyenne and Arapaho could not pay for newly acquired agricultural equipment.[38]

Several groups of Oklahoma Indians borrowed money to establish cooperative business associations. The Comanches received a loan of $1,750 to establish the Walters District Poultry Cooperative, a small number of Chickasaws borrowed money to raise peanuts, while Choctaw full bloods near Idabel started a cattle business. Several Cherokee families formed a strawberry cooperative at Lyons Switch. They received a loan of $2,800, paid back this debt, and each family earned an annual profit of $600. But the other cooperatives were plagued with financial problems which resulted in an 18 percent delinquency rate on their loans.[39]

Thirty-nine credit associations also were established to assist Indian farmers who lived on land allotments. In 1937 the Indian Bureau drew up a master plan which authorized the creation of county credit associations. Morris Opler, a member of the bureau's applied anthropology unit, discovered that the Creeks disliked this proposal. They wanted to set up credit associations based on tribal towns that had kept their identity since the Creek Confederacy. Opler reported this information to his superiors at the Indian Bureau but a shortage of anthropologists made it impossible to determine whether all of the Five Civilized Tribes wanted to organize along town lines. Local Indian Bureau officials also feared that Opler wanted to restore outmoded tribal customs, so they pushed ahead with the organization of county credit associations for the Five Civilized Tribes.[40]

The Oklahoma Welfare Act permitted all Indians on tribal rolls and their descendents to apply for loans from the credit associations. Applicants with only a trace of Indian blood quickly requested authority to organize associations, while the full bloods were generally slow in presenting their loan applications. The Indian Bureau tried to reverse this trend by requiring full security on loans for "essentially white people," while allowing full bloods to use a crop lien for collateral. The result was increased tension between full and mixed-bloods and default on payments by inexperienced individuals who were bad credit risks.[41]

By 1944 the government had committed over $686,000 to the credit associations but most of them had become insolvent or were in the process of liquidation. The credit associations were run by inexperienced and unsalaried personnel and they lacked outside income to cover financial losses. A substantial amount of money advanced to the Indians was used to pay for the high administrative costs to supervise a federal loan program. The failure of the Indians to meet deadlines for loan applications often resulted in bureaucratic delays of up to one year.[42]

In the eastern part of the state, the government employed only fifteen farm agents to help members of the Five Civilized Tribes manage their loans. This led to continued Indian apathy and economic deprivation. When the New Deal ended in 1945, the region east of the Grand River was "one vast slum." Most Indians in this area lived in "poverty-stricken hovels" and they were plagued with "disease, drunkenness, crime and general moral delinquency."[43]

Many Oklahoma Indians did not participate in credit associations, business cooperatives, or bother to establish tribal self-government, because they were more interested in settling their claims against the United States. When Congress failed to pass a claims bill in 1935, Joseph Bruner and other leaders of the American Indian Federation began a campaign to secure passage of a bill co-sponsored by Senator Elmer Thomas and Representative Usher Burdick of North Dakota. This legislation would have ended federal control over the restricted land allotments held by members of the AIF and provided a $3,000 cash settlement of their individual claims against the government.[44]

Congress failed to pass the Thomas-Burdick bill. Nevertheless, this legislation reflected the concerns of acculturated Oklahoma Indians who had joined pan-Indian groups such as the National Indian Confederacy, American Indian Federation, and the Association of Indian Tribes. All of these organizations opposed the Indian New Deal because it attempted to revive tribal cohesiveness that for the most part no longer existed in Oklahoma. These Indians preferred to continue the process of assimilation and become Indian Americans instead of American Indians. They wanted to settle their claims against the United States, lease or sell their land, work as wage laborers, and maintain a diminishing sense of tribal culture by holding pan-Indian powwows and other informal social affairs.[45]

The Oklahoma Indian New Deal never recovered from the crisis it faced in 1934 because the Indians had little voice in determining the federal policies that were imposed on them. Most tribesmen were bewildered by the Wheeler-Howard bill and they had little input into the final version of the Oklahoma Welfare Act. Government officials generally ignored their arguments about the need to honor past treaty commitments, provide a claims settlement, and organize credit associations along town lines.

Oklahoma Indians agreed with Collier when he quoted William Shakespeare at the Muskogee Congress in 1934 to demonstrate that they faced a turning point in their history. But they did not want to re-establish reservations that had been dismantled for almost fifty years. They were proud of their progress as citizens under difficult circumstances. Instead of turning to the past, they wanted to remain "Indians with thoughts and ideas of contemporary white citizens."[46]

Indian women with their own quilt work and canned goods for showing at a fair. The white child is Glen Becker, a relative of the photographer. (Courtesy Western History Collections, University of Oklahoma Library.)

Constitutions for the Indians:

Trials and Tribulations for the Kiowa, Comanche, and Apache

By Forrest D. Monahan, Jr.

For Oklahoma the 1930s were a time of tribulation and hope, trial and disappointment. This is apparent in three Indian tribes who had been closely associated since the eighteenth century. The Kiowa, Comanche, and the Kiowa-Apache alliance had developed during the best of the old buffalo days, had endured the defeats of the Plains Wars, and lasted on into the reservation period. The reserve set aside for them was in the southwest corner of what later became Oklahoma. By federal law and decisions enacted from 1887 to 1901 they were required to give up their lands and to accept individual farms of 160 acres. The excess land was then opened to whites. The policy of the federal government was to turn the Indians into farmers, but large obstacles hindered this course. The Indians' lack of experience in complex farming was a drawback, as were the reluctant soil and the uncertain weather. Nevertheless, the Bureau of Indian Affairs energetically pursued the policy.[1]

Superintendent J. S. Buntin, agent for the three tribes from 1922 to 1932, enthusiastically and doggedly followed the objective of turning the Indians into agriculturalists, and he had some success. Helping him was a small group of extension agents whose duties were to teach the Indians techniques of agriculture and cattle raising. With activities similar to those of white county extension agents they distributed bulletins and the latest information available. Also a part of this policy was sending women home demonstration agents to farm homes to instruct Indian wives on how to grow the best in gardens and how to can vegetables and cook sumptious repasts for their families. Home demonstration clubs were organized for the women and farm clubs for the men to facilitate the instruction. Buntin also urged the Indians to participate in the many county and regional fairs which took place in the early fall. He believed that the Indians could successfully compete with whites in these rural affairs where livestock and produce were displayed and judged. The Indians under his jurisdiction had notable success in the mid and late twenties, winning ribbons for excellence in livestock, grains, garden vegetables, and home canning. The local newspapers carefully reported on these accomplishments.[2]

However, near the end of his tour of duty, Buntin's policies suffered two challenges which brought them into question. One was nature-made, a severe drought, which was not easily dealt with. The other was man-made and unexpected, but nevertheless more easily managed. It came from the Reformed Presbyterian Church, a small fundamentalist group with whom Buntin had previously had good relations.[3]

The three tribes had experienced a growing familiarity with the Protestant churches of which the Methodist Church South, the Southern Baptist, and the Dutch Reformed had the most profound influence. The fact that these churches encouraged Indian ministers to preach and allowed a good deal of local congregational control seemed to fit the Indian outlook. Also facilitating Indian acceptance was the fact that the denominations came to an accommodation with the Native American Church, although somewhat uncomfortably so in the case of the Baptists. During the 1920s a late arrival, the Reformed Presbyterian Church, began a missionary effort among the Indians of southwestern Oklahoma, but it achieved only minor success compared to the more established denominations. By the spring of 1931 its missionaries had fixed the blame for their small success on local fairs and rodeos. In doing so they ran athwart of both the Bureau of Indian Affairs and the other churches as well.

The Indian participation in the fairs was dual. While taking part in agricultural competition, they also used nearby campgrounds which white fair sponsors set aside for this purpose. These colorful Indian camps of tents, tipis, and arbors were an established part of many country fairs. The tribesmen were encouraged to have Indian dances and display their own handicrafts such as beadwork and leatherwork. Thus the fairs, while encouraging agricultural participation, also were a means to further Indian culture. Kiowa, Comanche, and Kiowa-Apache visited with relatives and renewed old acquaintances. The camps were the scene of good-natured socializing and native dancing.

It was this native aspect that the Presbyterians hit upon as subversive of their programs. In the spring of 1931 the field missionaries alerted their eastern co-religionists to the dangers of paganism and immorality in southwestern Oklahoma, requesting them to bring pressure on Congress, the Indian Bureau, and the Department of Interior to halt what the Presbyterians called "picnics." They objected to the public fairs as well as the Indian fair privately sponsored by Frank Rush at Craterville, eighteen miles west of Lawton. Reformed Presbyterians responded with enthusiasm. Congress and the federal bureaucracy were deluged with letters, a few from Oklahoma, but most of them from the northeastern states. Mrs. Florence Tibby of Pittsburgh, Pennsylvania, wrote identical letters to the Secretary of

Interior and to the Commissioner of Indian Affairs, protesting the violation of laws at the "Indian picnics." The Reverend J. Clifford Matthews of Birmingham, Michigan, wrote to the Commissioner of Indian Affairs that the Indians practiced gross immorality and native ceremonials at the fairs, and consequently the government should forbid their participation. The Reverend Matthews also wrote an almost identical letter to the Secretary of the Interior.[4]

With both congressmen and executive departments receiving such protests clothed in terms of accepted public morality, the Indian Bureau reacted in a fashion that would protect itself and involve the Baptists, Methodists, and Dutch Reformed, who in fact were as much barriers to Presbyterian success as were the Indian fairs, although, of course, the Presbyterians could not make a direct assault on their fellow Christians. To deal with the charges the Commissioner of Indian Affairs authorized Superintendent Buntin to call a general conference of all churchmen and missionaries who worked among the three tribes as well as Indian Bureau officials whose duties were with the same tribes. The meeting included a number of tribesmen who were Baptist and Methodist ministers and also Indian laity. The Reformed Presbyterians were hopelessly outnumbered.[5]

agreed that religious issues had to be set in the context of life and culture. It made the simple observation that living conditions were important. It then spent most of its time on Indian health and economic problems. In its concluding resolutions the conference commended the Bureau and its goals of better farming, better education, and improved health measures. It also asserted that the county fairs were good places for Indians to show whites the results of their own work. While recognizing that "harmful practices" sometimes took place at fairs, it declared that the fairs offered more benefits than harm to the Indians. And then the council took a swipe at the Presbyterians for trying to achieve their aims through political pressure rather than through Christian persuasion; it urged each church and denomination to cooperate to improve the Indians' spiritual life by improving their education, health, and economic well-being. Buntin had been vindicated.[6]

The Presbyterian protest led to an unforeseen result, the writing of a constitution for the three tribes, the first of several in the 1930s. In dealing with the Presbyterians Superintendent Buntin and his aides had relied heavily on the Kiowa-Comanche-Apache Business Committee. In doing so the Bureau followed a long established practice of consulting Indian opinion. Though it might not like Indian

Kiowas in ceremonial costume. The occasion is a fair at Craterville. During most of the year these men would dress in white men's clothing. In the 1930s most white people found the Indians' wearing the elegant old time fashions to be interesting and even inspiring. However the Reformed Presbyterians, a small minority, were simply outraged. (Courtesy Western History Collections, University of Oklahoma Library.)

ideas on specific proposals it could not ignore Indian thought. In addition to samples gained in normal day-to-day activity there were three methods of normal consultation. One was an assembly of all three tribes, usually called a general council, in which all adult members could participate. To conduct business in a general council was awkward. The three tribes had about 4,500 members of whom several hundred would probably attend a meeting. But a disadvantage was the language problem, since all business had to be conducted in four languages—English, Comanche, Apache, and Kiowa—which considerably slowed the pace of the meeting and led to further problems of translation. Another type of council was the tribal council, in which the adult members of each tribe met separately. This would still involve large numbers of people for the Kiowa and Comanche. A further disadvantage was that it created suspicion among the Indians that the white bureaucrats would try to play one tribe against the other.[7]

So the Bureau had developed yet another means of consulting opinion: an elected business committee for the three tribes. As early as 1909, the Bureau had authorized the selection of such a committee, which was consultative only, but certainly easier to meet with than several hundred people speaking in four languages. There was no specific document or constitution which detailed the framework of the committee, the procedures being established entirely by correspondence, letters, and memoranda in the Bureau. However, the results of consultation between the business committee and the superintendent had been so effective in the recent Presbyterian controversy that both the Bureau and the Indians agreed that a more formal arrangement for a business committee was desirable. The result was the Kiowa, Comanche, and Apache Constitution of January, 1932.[8]

The new constitution was brief. Even with the authorizing signatures of Jasper Saunkeah, Kiowa, as Chairman, and Albert Attocknie, Comanche, as Secretary, it covered only one and one-third pages. It was also vague, not stating the term of office of members or the number of members to be appointed. Its powers were consultative only, but the requirement of monthly meetings clearly assumed close cooperation between the committee and the Bureau of Indian Affairs. The committee had no standing in law, since no law had authorized its creation, nor did the constitution receive the approval of the Commissioner of Indian Affairs. The document contained no new departures. It merely put in written form practices that already existed. It was also vague enough that these practices could be changed if the Bureau so desired.[9]

Events soon outdated this constitution. The same year it was written Franklin Roosevelt was elected President and

Kiowa and Comanche leaders with Senator Thomas P. Gore. The photographer has clearly marked the man next to Senator Gore as "Attocknie." (Courtesy Western History Collections, University of Oklahoma Library.)

his New Deal program inaugurated important governmental reforms. Indian policy was to undergo major change. John Collier, the new Commissioner of Indian Affairs, aimed to reverse the trends of the last four decades to destroy native culture. Idealistic and energetic, he proposed to reinvigorate tribal government and to stop the breakup of reservations. While reservations no longer existed in Oklahoma, the Collier policy intended to stop the erosion of Oklahoma Indian rights and to radically improve the economic well-being of native Americans.[10]

The first major New Deal law that attempted to reshape Indian government according to Collier policy was the Indian Reorganization Act of 1934, also known as the Wheeler-Howard Act. Since its terms dealt mostly with reservation issues, its major sections did not apply specifically to Oklahoma, because Indian reservations no longer existed there.[11] Thus it was necessary to write a special law applicable to the Indians of the Sooner State.

In the following months Senator Elmer Thomas, Chairman of the Senate Committee on Indian Affairs, and Congressman Will Rogers, Chairman of the House Indian Committee, both held hearings on Oklahoma Indian matters. In each committee Oklahoma Indians endorsed new bills prepared by Collier and the Indian Bureau.[12] This resulted in the Oklahoma Indian Welfare Act of 1936, also known as the Thomas-Rogers Act.[13]

The Collier plan was to take initiative out of the Bureau of Indian Affairs and to place more responsibility with the tribes. Though the Oklahoma tribes no longer had reserves, there were many areas of Indian rights and property where power for principal decisions lay with the Bureau; the Indians acted in merely advisory capacity. This meant that the Bureau could override Indian sentiment even when the decisions were not in the interests of the Indians. A series of events still vivid in the minds of many illustrated the near-autocratic power of the Bureau and its officers. These concerned the forced land patents, when Superintendent C. F. Stinchecum, Buntin's predecessor from 1915 to 1922, acting upon the directions of the Bureau, forced a number of Indians to take their land out of federal trust and accept titles in fee simple. This was done over the objections of the Business Committee, against tribal sentiment, and also over the objections of individual Indian owners, some of whom did not speak English. The unsoundness of the policy was clear. Untrained in taxes, property, or credit, many of the people soon lost their farms for taxes and debt. Moreover, they lost the land at less than its real value.[14] It was such outrageous actions that Collier hoped the Oklahoma Indian Welfare Act would end.

The key was section three of the act which would allow the Oklahoma tribes to write constitutions and to inaugurate business committees with the power to conduct tribal matters. The law also allowed the tribes to incorporate. The Thomas-Rogers Act was a major step forward in reviving Indian responsibility for Indian matters. Its purpose was to terminate the mere advisory status of tribal councils and business committees and to give them real authority. While not ending the supervisory function of the federal government it would curtail the dictatorial powers of the Bureau superintendents and require them to function with the tribal committees. While Collier had confidence in his own administration and workers, as a good bureaucrat he knew he would not always be in office and he wished to bind his successors to respect for tribal government by law.[15]

The procedure for inaugurating a constitution was only moderately complex. The purpose was to involve all elements affected: tribes, business committees, superintendents, and the Commissioner himself. The process began with a consultation between the Superintendent and tribe, and if there was sufficient sentiment for a constitution, a tribal business committee would write the document. The constitution would then go the Superintendent; if he approved, it would go to the Commissioner of Indian Affairs; if the Commissioner approved, the constitution would then go back to the tribe where the entire adult population voted in a secret ballot. Before it could go into effect a majority vote of approval was required. Collier and his advisors had carefully crafted this procedure so that it would involve the Indians at the beginning and end of the process. It reflected an almost populist belief in the benefits of democracy and open discussion.[16]

The Oklahoma Indian Welfare Act and its provisions for tribal constitutions seem to have clarified legal questions about the Kiowa-Comanche-Apache self-government, except that they already had a constitution; and it was not the 1932 constitution. The general optimism, instilled by the New Deal, added to the immense hopes generated by the trend for Indian reform, had moved the three tribes to write a new constitution in 1935. The latter document was more precise concerning the membership, elections, and terms of the business committee than was the 1932 endeavor. The Kiowa were to have four members, the Comanche four, and the Apache two, a distribution roughly proportional to each

A truck carrying Indians in traditional costume from camp to the ceremonial grounds. The mountain in the background indicates this is Craterville. (Courtesy Western History Collections, University of Oklahoma Library.)

tribe's population. Committeemen were to have two-year terms. Each tribe was to meet separately in December to elect members who were to take office the following January. As for the powers of the Business Committee, it was to cooperate with the government's wardship program, and work to improve health and educational opportunities. A vague phrase into which a number of meanings could be read said that the Business Committee was to "represent the tribes in all matters affecting the Kiowa, Comanche and Apache Indians." However, since this phrase was coupled with another in Article V, Section 2, which said the committee could investigate the Bureau of Indian Affairs, it seemed to have less to do with conducting such business as signing contracts and more to do with the committee's authority to investigate.[17]

The 1935 constitution was vague in many respects, but it was more clear than the 1932 constitution. Its major advantages were that it more precisely stated the methods of elections and the makeup of the committee. Its major disadvantage had little to do with its provisions, but rather its questionable legal status. The Wheeler-Howard Act, passed a few months previously and which allowed tribes to form governments, stated that this did not apply to Oklahoma (Section 13). And of course the Thomas-Rogers bill, which would allow the Oklahoma Indians to form business committees, had not yet passed the Congress. The Bureau of Indian Affairs had no clear authority to either approve or disapprove the 1935 constitution, and as a result the Bureau waited until Congress should declare policy in a specific act.

made two decisions which caused much controversy in the following months. First, it decided that the Thomas-Rogers Act had invalidated the 1935 constitution.[18] The second decision came not from the Bureau but from the intertribal business committee which asked that the three tribes be separated, so that each could have its own business committee. Superintendent Walter McCown, Buntin's successor, agreed to this request, perhaps unwisely in view of the confusion which attempted separation later caused. Each tribe formed "constitutional business committees" whose duties were to write constitutions. In consultation with their own tribesmen the committees proceeded to meet and to write in the spring and summer of 1937. The Comanche were the fastest. They gave their finished document to the Superintendent, who, approving it, sent it to the Commissioner, who also approved it. The constitution then went back to the Comanche for a full tribal vote. To the shock of McCown and the Indian Bureau the Comanche in August, 1937, defeated their own constitution, by a vote of 472 to 162.[19]

McCown was aware of Comanche objections but did not know that opposition was so strong. In fact the ratification issue was becoming a major political campaign dividing each of the three tribes into two political factions, one supporting the New Deal constitutions, the other opposed. After the Comanche election, the scene shifted to the Kiowa where sentiment was more evenly divided, and where also the contest was more open and the issues more publicly discussed. The results of the election which took place in December were 348 to 302 against adoption. Voting in their election a few weeks later in January, 1938, the Apache also defeated their constitution. The margin was indeed close. The constitution failed by one vote: 61 to 62.[20]

The three tribes' rejection of these constitutions was a blow to the prestige of the Indian service. Several issues blended together to cause the defeat. One was a confusion over the two major laws, the Indian Reform Act of 1934 and the Oklahoma Indian Welfare Act of 1936. The former act was designed primarily for reservations; and its emphasis on commonly held land by the tribe at the expense of individually-owned allotments disturbed many Oklahoma Indians. Members of the three tribes who still had allotments wanted to keep their individual land rather than turn it over to tribal ownership. The fact that the Oklahoma Act prohibited such confiscation did not reduce suspicion.[21]

An additional factor in the defeat was internal rivalry within the tribes, which seemed especially intense during the thirties. Positions on the business committees became matters of prestige and the object of campaigning. Groups not represented on the committees feared that the procedure would freeze their rivals in office. Two parts of the transition alarmed them. The first was the fact that the current committee members would remain in office until the end of 1937 and would therefore conduct the elections for the new committees; the second was Article VI, Section 2 of the Kiowa constitution which gave the new committee members four-year terms. Those out of power believed that these two factors together would keep their rivals in office for four long years.[22]

A special set of conditions applied to the Comanches, several of whom in Cotton County had organized a credit cooperative under the Oklahoma Welfare Act. They believed that the proposed constitution would nullify their association, even though the Act clearly allowed both tribal government and cooperatives to coexist.[23]

The confusion was evident in a congressional hearing which took place some time later. Representative Will Rogers, who helped to write the Thomas-Rogers Act along the lines of Indian wishes, was curious to learn why things happened as they did. The puzzled congressman asked Comanche tribesmen Tomah and Albert Attocknie why their tribe had turned down the 1937 constitution. Tomah replied that many voters misunderstood the issues. Tomah's answer could well apply to all three tribes.[24]

Additionally, the enthusiasm of the Bureau of Indian Affairs officials for the new constitutions was a negative factor in the minds of many Indians. Distrust and suspicion brought on by the past made many believe that what the Bureau wanted could not be of any good. Moreover the Bureau's attitude towards the 1935 constitution puzzled many. While the Bureau was on sound legal grounds when it held that the document had not been authorized by a specific congressional act, it did not make sense to many voters that they should twice within two years have to reorganize their tribal government. The entire thing smelled of trickery. In the fall of 1937 the more that McCown and his aides endorsed the proposed constitution, the more the Kiowa turned against it. And the separation of the intertribal business committee into three committees was a distinct break with the past that angered many. Then too, the suggestion for separation had come from the intertribal committee; it proved unpopular and the Bureau of Indian Affairs received the blame.[25]

The rejection of the three constitutions brought on an embarrassing situation. The terms of the old business committee members expired at the end of 1937, and elections could not take place under the 1937 constitutions, because these had been rejected. The automatic suspension of tribal government caught everyone by surprise. The Bureau had made no preparation for elections under the old procedure, believing that the new constitutions would be approved. As for the tribes, neither side appeared to want elections until the status of the proposed government was decided. Their attention was taken up in the ratification process. Neither the Bureau nor the Indians had contemplated the possibility of there being no tribal government.[26]

As the election smoke settled in 1938 the two sides among the Comanche, Apache, and Kiowa regrouped for further battle. One wanted to revive tribal government without reference to the Oklahoma Act. The other wanted to go ahead and organize under the Oklahoma Act even though they were a minority. Upon surveying the situation the Bureau decided that sentiments within the three tribes were too intense to risk an election. Another election so soon after the ratification campaign would further inflame opinion when a cooling-off period was needed. The Bureau concluded it would be better to continue for a while with self-government temporarily suspended.[27]

For three years the tribes were without tribal government, but this situation could not last indefinitely. Issues and conditions were developing that needed some sort of tribal

School girls at Cache Creek Indian Mission. They have put on traditional costume for a special occasion, probably just for the photographer. (Courtesy Western History Collections, University of Oklahoma Library.)

political body that would consult with the government and could also have the power to make contracts. Specifically, the tribes had claims against the government left over since the nineteenth century. To adjudicate these the government had set up a claims commission. It was necessary for the tribes to hire lawyers to investigate the claims and to argue before the commission. These were things the Bureau could not do. Technically an assembly of all tribesmen could make the decisions, but expecting several hundred people to meet monthly to consider such matters was unrealistic.[28]

Considering these issues in 1940 the Bureau decided it was necessary to re-create tribal government. Enough time had elapsed to allow partisan feelings to cool, and amongst the tribesmen themselves much sentiment existed to have a business committee of some sort. The question was how to do this. The answer was imaginative. Going back through its files the Bureau found copies of the 1932 and 1935 constitutions, both of which clearly had tribal approval. It ruled that the 1932 constitution was valid, and that the 1935 constitution was a valid amendment, even though it was longer than the 1932 document. This was creative bureaucracy. Thus eight years after the writing of one constitution and five years after the formulation of another the Bureau of Indian Affairs did exactly what Collier feared; it made broad decisions on Indian welfare without involving the Indians.[29]

The tribesmen in the meantime were bringing their influence to bear. Many told Superintendent McCown that they wanted to amend the 1935 constitution before it went into effect. Agreeing to this, the Bureau called for a general council of the three tribes.[30] The meeting took place at Riverside Indian School near Anadarko on October 10, 1940. After listening to a speech of greetings from Superintendent McCown, the council chose William Karty as chairman and James Daugomah as secretary for the day. Concluding that the tribes should remain allied, they rejected the proposed separation of 1937. They then moved through the 1935 constitution, paragraph by paragraph. Only four changes resulted from these deliberations. First, the number of Kiowa and Comanche representatives was increased from four to five each, the Apache delegates remaining at two. This was done on the grounds that it more accurately represented the proportional population of the tribes. There was no opposition to the proposal. The second change concerned the term of office. The council substituted a proposal from the rejected 1937 constitution, increasing the terms of committee members from two to four years. Third, they decided that the three business committee officers, chairman, vice-chairman, and secretary, should each be from different tribes. This was to guarantee that each tribe would have an officer (Article III, Section 2). The fourth change was to increase the required number for a quorum from one officer and six members to one officer and seven members. This was in accord with increasing the overall membership of the committee. Except for these alterations the council adopted the 1935 constitution almost word for word.[31]

The federal acceptance of the 1940 constitution closed a story that began with a Presbyterian protest against the Bureau's encouragement of native rights. That same acceptance also allowed the re-creation of tribal government along the lines of the 1935 constitution which of course pre-dated the proposed Collier constitutions by two years. This clearly indicated that the political fight over adoption in 1937 was unnecessary; on the other hand it justified Collier's view that tribal government was essential to the welfare of the Indians.

Notes

Depression Politics

[1] The material for this essay is drawn from the authors' larger study, a history of Oklahoma politics since statehood. It appears here with their special permission. They gratefully acknowledge the support of the National Endowment for the Humanities for grant RS-32318-78-838, which helped finance that larger work and this selection.

[2] An excellent study of the depression's effects is W. Richard Fassey, "'Talking' Dust Bowl Blues:' A Study of Oklahoma's Cultural Identity During the Great Depression," *The Chronicles of Oklahoma,* Volume LV, Number 1 (Spring, 1977), pp. 12-33. Also see H. Wayne Morgan and Anne Hodges Morgan, *Oklahoma: A Bicentennial History*, States and the Nation Series (New York: W. W. Norton for the American Association for State and Local History, 1977), pp. 161-70.

[3] The fullest account of the gubernatorial campaign, told from the vantage point of the eventual winner, is Francis W. Schruben, "The Return of Alfalfa Bill Murray," *The Chronicles of Oklahoma*, Volume XLI, Number 1 (Spring, 1963), pp. 38-65.

[4] William H. Murray, *Memoirs of Governor Murray and True History of Oklahoma,* 3 vols. (Boston: Meador Publishing Co., 1945), Vol. II, pp. 364-67; Keith L. Bryant, *Alfalfa Bill Murray* (Norman: University of Oklahoma Press, 1968), pp. 151-72, quotation from p. 177.

[5] On the metropolitan press, see Schruben, "Return of Alfalfa Bill Murray," pp. 41-44. Murray's reaction to a particularly vicious attack is recounted in his *Memoirs*, Vol. II, pp. 380.

[6] Murray carried fifty-four counties in building a lead of nearly two to one. Source: Oklahoma State Election Board, *Directory of Oklahoma, 1979*, p. 553.

[7] *Ibid.*, p. 556.

[8] Quoted in Bryant, *Alfalfa Bill Murray*, p. 190.

[9] The most vigorous charge of demagoguery is in Reinhard H. Luthin, *American Demagogues: Twentieth Century* (Boston: Beacon Press, 1954), pp. 102-26.

[10] County Relief Files, W. W. Redwine Collection, Western History Collections, University of Oklahoma, Norman, Oklahoma, hereinafter cited as WHC.

[11] Henry J. Bitterman, *State and Federal Grants-in-Aid* (New York and Chicago: Mentzner, Bush, & Co., 1938), p. 155.

[12] Bryant, *Alfalfa Bill Murray*, pp. 205, 246.

[13] Executive Proclamations Nos. 1709-1714, April 14, 1934, Secretary of State's Files, Oklahoma State Archives, Oklahoma City, Oklahoma; hereafter cited as State Files.

[14] Executive Proclamation No. 1729, July 30, 1934, State Files.

[15] *Daily Oklahoman*, March 12, 1932.

[16] Murray's initiative campaign took its name from the governor's warning to the 1931 legislature, that "the roll will be called and the firebells will be rung before this is over." The campaign took the form of seven state questions, four of which appeared at a special election in December, 1931, the remainder at the primary elections of July, 1932. In addition to the tax proposals, the questions included the escheat of corporate-owned land to the state and the provision of state-purchased textbooks for elementary school children.

[17] A good secondary account is available in William S. Harmon, "Oklahoma's Constitutional Amendments: A Study in the Use of the Initiative and Referendum" (Ph.D. diss., University of Oklahoma, 1951), pp. 124-30.

[18] Drawing upon the candidate's slogan, a campaign song featured such inspired verses as:

Give us the good old days, give us
  the good old days.
Give us the old familiar scenes.
Then we'll have money to pay the rent.
Murray for President.
Bread, Butter, Bacon, and Beans.

The ill-fated presidential quest is covered at length in Bryant, *Alfalfa Bill Murray*, pp. 214-36.
[19] FERA Files, William H. Murray Collection, Oklahoma State Archives, Oklahoma City, Oklahoma.
[20] The story is recounted in James T. Patterson, *The New Deal and the States: Federalism in Transition* (Princeton, N. J.: Princeton University Press, 1969), p. 54.
[21] Murray's ill-temper was undoubtedly worsened by the dismal performance of his handpicked slate. Of the ten candidates whom the outgoing governor had blessed, only two won nomination in the Democratic primary. Five placed second, and the remainder finished well down the list.
[22] *Directory of Oklahoma, 1979*, pp. 559, 563.
[23] For an admiring portrait that emphasized Marland's business career, see John Joseph Mathews, *Life and Death of an Oilman: The Career of E. W. Marland* (Norman: University of Oklahoma Press, 1951).
[24] *Oklahoma News*, January 8, 1935.
[25] The following paragraphs are taken from *Governor Marland's First Message to the Fifteenth Legislature, January 15, 1935*, copy in Oklahoma Governors Collection, Oklahoma State Archives, Oklahoma City, Oklahoma.
[26] Prior to his inauguration, Marland had privately commissioned the Brookings Institution to compile a report on the operations of Oklahoma government with recommendations for their thorough overhaul. *The Report of Survey of Organization and Administration of Oklahoma* was finally issued in mid-1935. The 483-page text was a thoughtful analysis of state and county government, including a battery of proposals for their improved operation. The proposals, like the *Report* itself, were conspicuously ignored by all save a few political scientists and, later, historians.
[27] *Harlow's Weekly*, February 16, 1935.
[28] The fate of Marland's program before the Fifteenth Legislature is fully covered in Cecil L. Turner, "Oklahoma's New Deal: Program and Reaction" (M.A. thesis, University of Oklahoma, 1963), pp. 7-34.
[29] Harmon, "Oklahoma's Constitutional Amendments," pp. 54-55.
[30] *Directory of Oklahoma, 1979*, pp. 649-50.
[31] *Associated Industries v. Oklahoma Tax Commission*, 176 Okla. 120 (1936).
[32] Harmon, "Oklahoma's Constitutional Amendments," pp. 61-62; Oklahoma Department of Welfare, *Fourth Annual Report of the Oklahoma Department of Welfare*, pp. 3-4.
[33] *Directory of Oklahoma, 1979*, pp. 566-77, 564.
[34] Turner, "Oklahoma's New Deal," pp. 64-106.
[35] *Harlow's Weekly*, Febrary 12, 1938; Beulah Elizabeth Amidon, "Sooners in Security: What is Happening in Oklahoma," *Survey Graphic*, April 1938, pp. 203-207. The sweeping federal indictment of the corrupt distribution is available in "Transcript of Hearings Before the Social Security Board," Clayton H. Hyde Collection, WHC.
[36] V. O. Key, *Southern Politics in State and Nation* (New York: Random House, Vintage Books, 1949), p. 16.

"Share the Work"

[1] Keith L. Bryant, Jr., "Oklahoma and the New Deal," in *The New Deal: The State and Local Levels* (Columbus: Ohio State University Press, 1976), pp. 167-168.
[2] *Ibid.*, p. 170.
[3] Author's interview with Ira Finley, April 16, 1979.
[4] Author's interview with Ira Finley, April 23, 1979.
[5] Bryant, "Oklahoma and the New Deal," p. 173.
[6] Author's interview with Ira Finley, April 16, 1979.
[7] Aubrey Williams to Harry Hopkins, June 30, 1933, Harry Hopkins Papers, container 59, Franklin D. Roosevelt Library, Hyde Park, New York, hereinafter cited as FDR Library.
[8] Author's interview with Ira Finley, April 16, 1979.
[9] *Oklahoma City Times*, October 5, 1932.
[10] Author's interview with Ira Finley, April 23, 1979.
[11] Facsimile of VIA Blue Card in author's possession.
[12] William J. Plunkert to Harry Hopkins, December 7, 1933. Harry Hopkins Papers, Container 59, FDR Library.
[13] *Ibid.*
[14] Author's interview with Ira Finley, April 23, 1979.
[15] *Ibid.*
[16] *VIA Voice*, September 7, 1934.
[17] *Ibid.*, January 1, 1934.
[18] *Labor's Voice*, November 9, 1934.
[19] *Ibid.*, July 26, 1935.
[20] *Daily Oklahoman*, September 18, 1935.
[21] Author's interview with Ira Finley, April-May, 1979.
[22] *Labor's Voice*, February 21, 1936.
[23] *Daily Oklahoman*, October 6, 1936.
[24] Author's interview with Herbert Finley, Sept. 12, 1979.
[25] Author's interview with Ira Finley, April-May, 1979.
[26] Author's interview with Winifred Brown, Aug. 9, 1979.
[27] *Labor's Voice*, August 23, 1935.
[28] Author's interview with Winifred Brown, Aug. 9, 1979.
[29] Author's interview with G. A. Ramsey, July 10, 1979.
[30] *Labor's Voice*, November 1, 1935.
[31] *Ibid.*, November 29, 1935.
[32] *Ibid.*, August 21, 1936.
[33] *Ibid.*, April 7, 1937.
[34] *Ibid.*, April 21, 1937.
[35] *Ibid.*
[36] Hopkins's appointment calendar, June 11, 1937, Hopkins Papers, Container 105, FDR Library.
[37] Author's interview with Ira Finley, April 23, 1979.
[38] *Ibid.*
[39] *Labor's Voice*, February 17, 1938.
[40] Leo Winters (comp.), *Directory of the State of Oklahoma* (Oklahoma City: State Election Board, 1959), p. 56.
[41] *Labor's Voice*, June 27, 1939.
[42] *Ibid.*, October n.d., 1940.
[43] *Daily Oklahoman*, December 29, 1940.
[44] *Ibid.*, February 2, 1941.
[45] *General Welfare Reporter*, September 8, 1942.
[46] *Ibid.*, March 15, 1947.
[47] Ira Finley died May 14, 1981, in Oklahoma City, Oklahoma, at the age of 94.

Hard Times for Children

[1] A. J. McLaughlin, "A Public Health Survey of Oklahoma," *Public Health Reports*, XLVI (March 13, 1931), pp. 575-598.
[2] *Ibid.*
[3] Bureau of the Census, *Mortality Statistics, 1930: Thirty-First Annual Report* (Washington, 1934), p. 3.
[4] Bernice N. Crockett, *The Origins and Development of Public Health in Oklahoma, 1830-1930* (Durant, Oklahoma: n.p., 1953), p. 178.
[5] Bureau of the Census, *Fifteenth Census of the United States: 1930, Population*, Vol. III pt. 2 (Washington, 1932), pp. 542, 564.
[6] Oklahoma Department of Public Health, "Public Health In Oklahoma," (1938) typescript, map no. 5, Oklahoma State University Library.
[7] *Public Health Reports*, LVII (October 2, 1942), p. 1494.
[8] R. N. Whitefield, "Problems in Rural Registration," *American Journal of Public Health and the Nation's Health*, XXVI (July, 1936), pp. 725-729: Bureau of the Census, *Vital Statistics Rates in the United States, 1900-1940* (Washington, 1943), p. 99.
[9] Bureau of the Census, *Vital Statistics of the United States 1937*, pt. 1 (Washington, 1939), pp. 30, 32; "Public Health in Oklahoma," map no. 5, typescript.
[10] Bureau of the Census, *Mortality Statistics, 1930*, pp. 268, 432; Bureau of the Census, *Vital Statistics of the United States, 1939*, pt. 1 (Washington, 1941), p. 305.
[11] *Ibid.*, p. 304; *Mortality Statistics, 1930*, p. 432; Bureau of the Census, *Vital Statistics of the United States 1933*, pt. 1 (Washington, 1936), p. 315; *ibid., Vital Statistics of the United States 1937*, pt. 1 (Washington, 1939), pp. 249-395.
[12] *Mortality Statistics, 1930*, p. 432; D. Clayton Brown, "Health of Farm Children in the South, 1900-1950," *Agricultural History*, LIII (January, 1979), p. 183.
[13] Wesley W. Spink, *Infectious Diseases: Prevention and Treatment in the Nineteenth and Twentieth Centuries* (Minneapolis: University of Minnesota Press, 1978), pp. 247-254.
[14] John Duffy, *Epidemics in Colonial America* (Baton Rouge: Louisiana State University Press, 1953), pp. 13-118; Crockett, *Origin and Development of Public Health in Oklahoma* , p. 212; *Public Health Reports* (March 13, 1931), p.590.
[15] Spink, *Infectious Diseases*, p. 197.
[16] *Vital Statistics 1937*, pp. 249-395.
[17] *Public Health Reports*, LV (May 10, 1940), p. 837.
[18] Brown, "Health of Farm Children in the South," p. 179.
[19] *Mortality Statistics 1930*, p. 433; *Vital Statistics 1937*, p. 352.
[20] For an excellent history of pellagra, see Elizabeth Etheridge, *The Butterfuly Caste: A Social History of Pellagra* (Westport, Connecticut: Greenwood Press, 1972).
[21] Brown, "Health of Farm Children in the South," p. 177.
[22] A. W. von Strave, "Better Rural Sanitation Improving Nation's Health," *Rural Sociology*, V (June, 1940), pp. 239-240.
[23] Brown, "Health of Farm Children in the South," pp. 184-185.
[24] State Department of Public Health, *Tenth Annual Report for the Fiscal Years 1928-29 and 1929-30* (Oklahoma City, 1930), pp. 15, 17-18.
[25] *Period Reports of Physical Examinations, Summary and Detailed Reports*, III, Selective Service Records, National Archives, Record Group, 147.
[26] "Health and Medical Care for Children," Submitted to the White House Conference on Children in a Democracy by the Children's Bureau, pamphlet (January 18-20, 1940, Washington, D.C.) pp. 168-171.

Dust, Farmers, and the Federal Government

[1] James Ware, "Concerning Grapes, Ballads, and Plows: the Cultural Impact of the Dust Bowl," (unpublished manuscript in hands of author); Alfred B. Sears, "The Desert Threat in the Southern Great Plains," *Agricultural History*, XV (January 1941), pp. 1-11; W. I. Drummond, "Dust Bowl," *Review of Reviews*, (June 1936), pp. 37-40.

[2] Harry C. McDean, "The 'Okie' Migration as a Social-Economic Necessity in Oklahoma," *Red River Valley Historical Review*, III (Winter 1978), p. 78; see Donald E. Green, "Beginnings of Wheat Culture in Oklahoma," in Donald E. Green ed., *Rural Oklahoma* (Oklahoma Historical Society: Oklahoma City, 1977), pp. 56-73.

[3] Agricultural Adjustment Administration, *Industry's Production Policy and the Farmer*, G-44 (Washington: Government Printing Office, September 1933), p. 1.

[4] C. Roger Lambert, "Hoover and the Red Cross in the Arkansas Drought of 1930," *The Arkansas Historical Quarterly* XXXIX (Spring 1970), pp. 3-19; *Daily Oklahoma*, September 2, 4, 7, 1930; Nan Elizabeth Woodruff, "The Great Southern Drought of 1930-31: A Study in Rural Relief," (unpublished dissertation, University of Tennessee, 1977).

[5] William R. Johnson, "Farm Policy in Transition: 1932, Year of Crisis," (unpublished dissertation, University of Oklahoma, 1963), pp. 65, 100; C. Roger Lambert, "Herbert Hoover and Federal Farm Board Wheat," *Heritage of Kansas*, X (1977), p. 27. Also see: Gilbert C. Fite, "John A. Simpson: The Southwest's Militant Farm Leader," *Mississippi Valley Historical Review*, XXXV (March, 1949), pp. 563-584.

[6] Grady Kennedy to Thomas, May 20, 1932; Henry G. Stowers to Thomas, March 28, 1933; W. J. McLoughlin to Thomas, April 3, 1933; John F. Bange to Thomas March 23, 1933; Elmer Thomas Collection, Western History Collection, University of Oklahoma, Norman, Oklahoma, hereinafter cited as WHC.

[7] T. M. Kirk to Elmer Thomas, September 17, 1933; Gore to Henry Wallace September 14, 1933; Trent to C. W. Warburton, October 5, 1933; Trent to Henry Wallace, August 23, 1933, Record Group 145, National Archives, Washington, D.C., hereinafter cited as RG 145, NA.

[8] Fred Floyd, "The History of the Dust Bowl," (unpublished dissertation, University of Oklahoma, 1951); pp. 28-37; *Tulsa Daily World*, January 16; April 24, 26, 30; May 23; June 8, 9, 20, 21, 26; July 13, 17, 18; November 3, 1933.

[9] Johnson, "Farm Crisis," p. 56; *Tulsa Daily World*, March 26, 1933.

[10] Floyd, "Dust Bowl," pp. 55-56.

[11] Lorena Hickok to Harry Hopkins, September 15, 1934, Hopkins Papers, Franklin D. Roosevelt Library, Hyde Park, New York (hereafter FDR Library). Hickok was a reporter, an investigator for Hopkins, and head of the Federal Emergency Relief Administration. She made this report from just across the boundary in Kansas and it came in 1934, but it seems to express the spirit of the Oklahoma farmer at least through 1934.

[12] Floyd, "Dust Bowl," pp. 68-69.

[13] *Tulsa Daily World*, March 26; May 10, 11, 15; June 1, 10, 11, 12, 21; July 2, 12, 15, 16; August 12, 16, 20, 28; September 9; *Daily Oklahoman*, July 11; September 9, 11; October 2, 3, 28, 1934.

[14] *Tulsa Daily World*, August 12, 1934.

[15] "The Drought of 1934-35: A Record of Programs of Commodities Purchase Section, Agricultural Adjustment Administration and Related Activities in Drought Stricken Areas," pp. 3-9, 65-68, 83-88 (unpublished manuscript, Statistical and Historical Unit, AAA) Records of Agricultural Stabilization and Conservation Service, RG 145 NA; *Daily Oklahoman*, July 2, 9, 1934.

16 C. Roger Lambert, "Texas Cattlemen and the AAA: 1933-1935," *Arizona and the West*, XIV (Summer 1972); pp. 137-154.
17 Michael Wayne Schuyler, "Agricultural Relief Activities of the Federal Government in the Middle West, 1933-1936," (unpublished dissertation, University of Kansas, 1969), p. 184; C. Roger Lambert, "The Drought Cattle Purchase, 1934-1935; Problems and Complaints," *Agricultural History* XLV (April 1971), pp. 85-94; Harry Petrie, Memorandum: "Reasons for Purchasing More Cattle under the Emergency Cattle Program," November 8, 1934, RG 145, NA.
18 Lambert, "Drought Cattle Purchases," pp. 88-90; "Texas Cattlemen," pp. 145-147; "The Drought of 1934-35," pp. 132, 185, 246.
19 Irvin M. May, "Cotton and Cattle: the FSRC and Emergency Work Relief," *Agricultural History* XLVI (July 1972), pp. 401-413; *Tulsa Daily World*, August 9, 22, 26, 28, 28; *Daily Oklahoma*, July 2, 9, 1934.
20 *Daily Oklahoma*, July 1, 1934.
21 Floyd, "Dust Bowl," p. 85; *Tulsa Daily World*, September 30; November 21; December 15, 1935.
22 *Tulsa Daily World*, March 17, 21, 1935; Floyd, "Dust Bowl," p. 85; *Tulsa Daily World*, August 24, 1936.
23 Telephone Transcript, Malcolm Miller with Mr. Williams, July 21, 1936, OF, FDRL: *Tulsa Daily World*, March 27, April 16, May 18, July 11, August 27, 28, 1936.
24 Floyd, "Dust Bowl," pp. 169-174.
25 *Tulsa Daily World*, March 22, May 27, 1936; Floyd, "Dust Bowl," pp. 130-131.
26 *Tulsa Daily World*, May 27, 1936.
27 *Ibid.*, May 12, 27; February 19, 1936.
28 *Ibid.*, May 12, October 23, 1936.
29 Floyd, "Dust Bowl," p. 119; *Tulsa Daily World*, May 12, October 23, 1936; Walter J. Stein, *California and the Dust Bowl Migration* (Westport, Connecticut: Greenwood Press, 1973), pp. 3-47; McDean, "The 'Okie' Migration," pp. 77-91. McDean argues that the transient problem existed in Oklahoma before the Great Depression and was one of the reasons for the poor state of farm life and that removal of many tenants was necessary to improvement for farmers in the state.
30 Roosevelt, Memorandum for Aubrey Williams, no date, OF, FDRL.
31 Rexford Tugwell, Memorandum to Roosevelt, December 4, 1935, OF, FDRL.
32 Report of the Great Plains Drought Area Committee, August, 1936; Summary of the final Report of the Great Plains Committee on the Future of the Great Plains, no date, Lyle T. Alverson to Roosevelt, August 12, 1936; summary of letter of Elmer Thomas, February 18, 1937, OF, FDRL; Ben Hibbs, "The Dust Bowl Can Be Saved," *The Saturday Evening Post*, CCX (December 18, 1937), pp. 16-17, 78, 80-82; Walter Davenport, "Land Where our Children Die," *Collier's*, C, September 13, 1937, pp. 12-13, 73-77.
33 Transcript, Presidential Drought Conference for Oklahoma, Des Moines, Iowa, September 3, 1936, OF FDRL; *Tulsa Daily World*, September 3-14, 1936.
34 Floyd, "Dust Bowl," p. 188.
35 *Amarillo Daily News* January 19, 1936; R. Douglas Hurt, "Agricultural Technology in the Dust Bowl, 1932-1940," paper read at Cultural Heritage of the Great Plains Symposium, April 15, 1977, Lincoln, Nebraska; Floyd, "Dust Bowl," pp. 162-167.
36 E. J. Kyle, "Important Changes in our Livestock Industry," *The Cattlemen*, XXVI (July 1940), pp. 25, 27.
37 *Daily Oklahoman*, November 17, 1940.

"We've Got the Hoover Blues"

[1] Harry C. McDean, "The 'Okie' Migration as a Socio-Economic Necessity in Oklahoma," *Red River Valley Historical Review*, III (Winter, 1978), p. 78.
[2] Jacqueline Gordon Sherman, "The Oklahomans in California During the Depression Decade, 1931-1941" (unpublished Ph.D. dissertation, University of California, Los Angeles, 1970), p. 47.
[3] *Ibid.*
[4] Donald W. Whisenhunt, "The Transient in the Depression," *Red River Valley Historical Review*, I (Spring, 1974), pp. 7-20; Thomas Minehan, *Boy and Girl Tramps of America* (Seattle: University of Washington Press, 1976 [reprint of 1934 edition with a new introduction by Donald W. Whisenhunt]).
[5] Donald W. Whisenhunt, "The Jobless Party in New Mexico," *The Greater Llano Estacado Southwest Heritage*, VIII (Spring, 1978), pp. 13-19.
[6] Santa Fe *New Mexican*, July 1, 1933.
[7] McDean, "The 'Okie' Migration," p. 87.
[8] Fred Floyd, "A History of the Dust Bowl" (unpublished Ph.D. dissertation, the University of Oklahoma, Norman, 1950), p. 119.
[9] Sherman, "Oklahomans in California," pp. 33, 47.
[10] *Ibid.*, p. 10.
[11] McDean, "The 'Okie' Migration," p. 87.
[12] *Ibid.*, p. 88.
[13] Sherman, "Oklahomans in California," ix, p. 22.
[14] *Ibid.*, p. 32.
[15] *Ibid.*, p. 24.
[16] "The Rig Builder," *Such as Us: Sourthern Voices of the Thirties*, edited by Tom E. Terrill and Jerrold Hirsch (Chapel Hill: The University of North Carolina Press, 1978), pp. 190-204.
[17] McDean, "The 'Okie' Migration," p. 91.
[18] Sherman "Oklahomans in California," p. 22.
[19] *Ibid.*, p. 37.
[20] *Ibid.*, ix.
[21] McDean, "The 'Okie' Migration," p. 77.
[22] Sherman, "Oklahomans in California," p. 23.
[23] *Ibid.*, pp. 31-37.
[24] As quoted in *ibid.*, p. 36.
[25] Studs Terkel, *Hard Times: An Oral History of the Great Depression* (New York: Pantheon Books, 1970), p. 48.
[26] Floyd, "History of the Dust Bowl," p. 59.
[27] Caroline A. Henderson, "Letters From the Dust Bowl," *The Atlantic Monthly*, CLVIII (May, 1936), pp. 540-551.
[28] McDean, "The 'Okie' Migration," p. 87.
[29] Sherman, "Oklahomans in California," p. 191.
[30] *Ibid.*, p. 113.
[31] Unidentified poem from Oklahoma, Democratic National Committee Correspondence, 1928-1933, Franklin D. Roosevelt Library, Hyde Park, New York, Box 631, hereinafter cited as FDR Library.
[32] Poem by W. E. Moxley, November 9, 1932, *ibid.*, Box 628.
[33] Poem by Geo. W. Bilbo, undated, *ibid.*, Box 631.
[34] David Eugene Conrad, *The Forgotten Farmers: The Story of Share Croppers in the New Deal* (Urbana: University of Illinois Press, 1965, p. 173.
[35]Sherman, "Oklahomans in California," pp. 34, 189.
[36] *Ibid.*, pp. 33, 190.
[37] *Ibid.*, pp. 280-281.
[38] *Ibid.*, pp. 72, 139.

"Jobs for Students"

[1] Keith L. Bryant, "Oklahoma and the New Deal," in Braeman, Bremner and Brody, *The New Deal: The State and Local Levels*, Vol. II (Columbus: Ohio State University Press, 1975), pp. 166-167. Also see: "Final Report: National Youth Administration for State of Oklahoma" (Unpublished manuscript, 1943), National Youth Administration, Oklahoma, Record Group 119, National Archives, Washington, D.C. Hereinafter cited: "Final Report."
[2] "Final Report," pp. 6-8.
[3] *Ibid.*, p. 9. Also see: Willard E. Givens, "New Deal A Raw Deal for the Public Schools," *Journal of the National Educational Association* (September, 1935), p. 198.
[4] "Final Report," p. 11; Houston Wright to John J. Corson, September 30, 1935; Wright to Richard Brown, October 9, 1935; October 31, 1935, December 11, 1935; Aubrey Williams to Wright, October 2, 1935; National Youth Administration, Oklahoma, Record Group 119, National Archives, Washington D.C. Hereinafter cited: NYA Okla RG 119 NA. Also see: *The Daily Oklahoman*, June 27, 1935.
[5] Aubrey Williams, "Roosevelt's Youth Program," *Current Controversy* (October, 1935), p. 6. Russell Eljoy to Wright, January 6, 1936, NYA Okla RG 119 NA.
[6] Wright to Brown, October 31, 1935; NYA Okla RG 119 NA.
[7] "Final Report," pp. 66-73.
[8] Ruth Alexander to A. H. Parmelee, May 4, 1936; NYA Okla RG 119 NA.
[9] Parmelee to Richard Brown, May 5, 1936; NYA Okla RG 119 NA.
[10] A. O. Martin, Director of Placement, Oklahoma A&M to Richard Brown, March 26, 1936; Shiller Scroggs, Dean, Oklahoma A&M, to Brown, March 27, 1936; John W. Raley, President, Oklahoma Baptist University, to Brown, May 7, 1936; Wright to Brown, October 14, 1936; Oscar D. Hutton, Jr., Langston University, to Wright, March 24, 1936; NYA Okla RG 119 NA.
[11] Report of the National Youth Administration School Work Council, n.d., Report of the National Youth Administration College Work Council, n.d.; Asa Keith, Field Work Director, School Work Council, to The Council, May 5: NYA Okla RG 119 NA.
[12] "Final Report," pp. 21-22.
[13] *Ibid.*, p. 23.
[14] *Ibid.*, pp. 25-29.
[15] *Ibid.*, p. 28.
[16] Houston Wright to Richard Brown, February 1, 1936; March 14, 1936; April 18, 1936; May 18, 1936; July 20, 1936; NYA Okla RG 119 NA.
[17] "Final Report," pp. 33-36. Wright to Brown, December 11, 1935; October 18, 1937; Mary H.S. Hayes to X, January 24, 1942; NYA Okla RG 119 NA.
[18] "Final Report," pp. 37-38; Lucille Hill, State Health Superintendent, to Dr. C. E. Rice, National Youth Administration Health Consultant, April 7, 1941; Dillard B. Lasseter, Deputy Administrator, National Youth Administration, to Bruce Carter, Oklahoma State Youth Director, February 10, 1941; Carter to Rice, June 17, 1942; Carter to Oscar H. Jones, National Youth Administration Resident Project Director, Seattle, Washington, June 19, 1942; NYA Okla RG 119 NA.
[19] Houston Wright to Richard Brown, November 6, 1936; NYA Okla RG 119 NA.
[20] Lawrence Burr, Oklahoma State Superintendent of Negro Affairs, to Mary McLeod Bethune, March 31, 1937; April 8, 1937; Richard Brown to Houston Wright, April 20, 1937; Brown to Burr, April 20, 1937; NYA Okla RG 119 NA.
[21] Report of Anne L. Caution to National Youth Administration National Office, March 21, 1939; NYA Okla RG 119 NA.
[22] Oklahoma City *Black Dispatch*, February 18, 1939; Report of Anne L. Caution to NYA National Office, March 21, 1939; NYA Okla RG 119 NA.
[23] "Final Report," pp. 50-51.

[24] Madill *Record*, February 15, 1937.
[25] Watonga *Republican*, March 25, 1937.
[26] Pauls Valley *Daily Democrat*, May 2, 1938.
[27] *The Daily Oklahoman*, August 8, 1936.
[28] Jed Johnson to Richard Brown, August 22, 1936; Brown to Johnson, September 17, 1936; NYA Okla RG 119 NA.
[29] Aubrey Williams to Houston Wright, September 14, 1939, NYA Okla RG 119 NA; Baltimore *Sun*, July 8, 1941.
[30] Irwin Ross, "Squeeze Play on Youth," *Thresehold* (December, 1941), pp. 20-22.
[31] *Congressional Record*, Vol. 87, Pt. 5, 77th Cong., 1st Sess. 4701; 5300; 5309; Pt. 8, 77th Cong., 1st Sess., 8734; Pt. 9, 77th Cong., 1st Sess., 914; Pt. 14, 77th Cong. 1st Sess., A 5303-08; A 5621.
[32] *United State Statutes at Large*, Vol. LV, "Final Report," pp. 40-42.
[33] *Congressional Record*, Vol. 88, Pt. 4, 77th Cong., 2nd Sess., 4828-46; 4905-20; 4926-68; 5596-5613; Pt. 5, 77th Cong., 2nd Sess., 5990.
[34] "Final Report," pp. 48-49.
[35] Duncan *Daily Democrat*, June 2, 1943.
[36] Washington *Post*, April 16, 17, 1942.
[37] Mabel Bassett to Aubrey Williams, April 15, 1942; NYA Okla RG 119 NA.
[38] Willard E. Givens to the Presidents of all State Educational Associations, May 27, 1943; NYA Okla RG 119 NA.
[39] "Should NYA Training be Turned Over to the Public Schools?" (Unpublished Manuscript, 1943); "Why the Schools Cannot Administer the NYA Training Program" (Unpublished Manuscript, 1943), NYA Okla RG 119 NA.
[40] *Congressional Record*, Vol. 89, Pt. 5, 78th Cong., 1st Sess., 6957-6969.
[41] *Ibid.*, pp. 7082, 7089.
[42] *The Daily Oklahoman*, July 5, 1943.
[43] "Final Report," pp. 38-39, 74-77.

For Better of For Worse

[1] Portions of this article appeared in Donovan L. Hofsommer, *Katy Northwest: The Story of a Branch Line Railroad* (Boulder, Colorado: Pruett Publishing, 1976).
[2] Carl Coke Rister, *No Man's Land* (Norman: University of Oklahoma Press, 1948), p. 191; W. H. Wells, former BM&E cashier at Hooker, Oklahoma, personal interview with the author, June 1, 1972; Vance Johnson, *Heaven's Tableland: The Dust Bowl Story* (New York: Farrar, Straus and Company, 1947), p. 147, 149-150; Charles Books Lewis, "The Development of Cimarron County" (unpublished M. A. thesis, University of Oklahoma, 1939), p. 66, 67.
[3] M-K-T Employees' Magazine, Vol. 19 (August 1931), pp. 4, 6, 48; E. B. Parks, former M-K-T agent, Mangum, Oklahoma, personal interview with the author, November 15, 1972.
[4] E. B. Parks interview, November 15, 1972; Johnson, *Heaven's Tableland*, p. 150; *Hooker Advance*, November 3, 1932.
[5] *Alva Review*, April 11, 1895; *Hooker Advance*, Pictorial Edition n. d. (1928); BM&E, Right-of-Way maps, Valuation Engineer's office, M-K-T, Denison, Texas; Johnson, *Heaven's Tableland*, pp. 169-170.
[6] Johnson, *Heaven's Tableland*, pp. 169-170; Rister, *No Man's Land*, pp. 181-183; Johnson, *Heaven's Tableland*, p. 173; *A History of Beaver County*, I, p. 314; *The Tulsa Tribune*, April 2, 1935.
[7] John W. Morris, *Oklahoma Geography* (Oklahoma City: Harlow Publishing Company, 1954), p. 39; Lewis, "Development of Cimarron County," pp. 67-68; Johnson, *Heaven's Tableland*, pp. 185-189; Rister, *No Man's Land*, pp. 182-185; *The Tulsa Tribune*, April 2, 1935.
[8] Mrs. Ruby Risen, former CRI&P agent at Baker, Oklahoma, November 15, 1972, to the author; Caroline A. Henderson, "Letters from the Dust Bowl," *The Atlantic Monthly*, Vol. 157 (May 1939), pp. 540-549; *The Tulsa Tribune*, April 2, 1935.

[9] Henderson, "Letters from the Dust Bowl," pp. 185-189; Hugh H. Parks, former BM&E section foreman at Hooker, Oklahoma, personal interview with the author, June 17, 1972.
[10] Henderson, "Letters from the Dust Bowl," pp. 541, 547.
[11] *Ibid.*
[12] Johnson, *Heaven's Tableland*, pp. 195, 206-207, 214, 216, 256; Rister, *No Man's Land*, p. 185.
[13] George W. Crosby, former BM&E engineer at Forgan, Oklahoma, personal interview with the author, November 16, 1972.
[14] Earl Walker, *The Fighting Railroad Mayor* (Boulder, Colorado: Johnson Publishing Company, 1968), pp. 110-111.
[15] *Ibid.*; Hugh H. Parks, personal interview with the author, January 17, 1973; E. B. Parks, personal interview with the author, November 15, 1972.
[16] Walker, *The Fighting Railroad Mayor*, p. 108.
[17] BM&E Employees' Time Table No. 24, May 14, 1939; Byron Bates, former M-K-T engineer at Elk City, Oklahoma, personal interview with the author, November 10, 1972.
[18] Hugh H. Parks, personal interview with the author, June 27, 1972.
[19] *Hooker Advance*, March 26, 1931; George W. Crosby, personal interview with the author, June 27, 1972.
[20] Rister, *No Man's Land*, p. 187; Johnson, *Heaven's Tableland*, p. 274; Morris, *Geography of Oklahoma*, pp. 149-150; U.S. Department of Commerce, Bureau of Census, "Year of Maximum Population by Counties of the United States," Map G. E.—50, No. 37 (Washington: U.S. Government Printing Office, 1971); Rister, *No Man's Land*, p. 191.

Indian Reform in Crisis

[1] For biographical background on the career of John Collier before he became Commissioner of Indian Affairs consult Kenneth R. Philp, *John Collier's Crusade for Indian Reform 1920-1954* (Tucson: University of Arizona Press, 1977), pp. 1-112.
[2] Proceedings of the Conference for the Indians of the Five Civilized Tribes of Oklahoma, Muskogee, Oklahoma, March 22-23, 1934, p. 45, Record Group 75, National Archives. (cited hereafter as RG 75 NA).
[3] U. S. Congress, House, Committee on Indian Affairs, *Hearings, on H.R. 6234, To Promote The General Welfare Of The Indians Of Oklahoma*, 74th Cong., 1st Sess., 1935, pp. 10-11, 205; and The Purpose and Operation of the Wheeler-Howard Indian Rights Bill, February 19, 1934, Hugh Scott Papers, Library of Congress.
[4] *Ibid.*
[5] H.R. 7902, A bill to grant Indians living under Federal tutelage, the freedom to organize for purposes of local self-government and economic enterprise, to provide the necessary training of Indians in administrative and economic affairs; to conserve and develop Indian lands, and to promote more effective justice in matters affecting Indian tribes and communities by establishing a Federal Court of Indian Affairs, February 12, 1934, Records Concerning the Wheeler-Howard Act, RG 75 NA.
[6] Meeting of Superintendent W. B. McCown with the Comanche Indians at the Fort Sill Indian School, Lawton, Oklahoma, March 12, 1934, RG 75 NA, Fort Worth Federal Records Center.
[7] Meeting of Superintendent W. B. McCown with the Kiowa Indians at Carnegie, Oklahoma, March 13, 1934, RG 75 NA, Fort Worth Federal Records Center.
[8] Meeting of the Commissioner of Indian Affairs, John Collier, with the Indians of Western Oklahoma at Anadarko, Oklahoma, March 20, 1934, pp. 4-8, RG 75 NA, Fort Worth Federal Records Center.

[9] *Ibid.*
[10] *Ibid.*, pp. 32, 43-47.
[11] *Ibid.*, pp. 51-58.
[12] Proceedings of the Conference for the Indians of the Five Civilized Tribes of Oklahoma, Muskogee, Oklahoma, March 22-23, 1934, p. 67, RG 75 NA, Fort Worth Federal Records Center.
[13] Statement by John Collier for the Press, May 24, 1934, Private Papers of John Collier, Yale University Library, New Haven, Connecticut.
[14] U.S. Congress, House, Committee on Indian Affairs, *Hearings, On H.R. 7781, Indian Conditions and Affairs*, 74th Cong., 1st Sess., 1935, pp. 863-869.
[15] The full blood Cherokees who belonged to the Night Hawk Keetoowah Society passed a resolution at Muskogee in favor of the Wheeler-Howard bill. Proceedings of the Conference of the Five Civilized Tribes of Oklahoma, March 22-23, 1934, pp. 7-14, 21-23, 25-30, 37-38.
[16] Minutes of the Meeting Held at Miami, Oklahoma, March 24, 1934, pp. 1-3, 12-16, Records Relating to the Wheeler-Howard bill, RG 75 NA.
[17] *Ibid.*, pp. 64-65, 73-74.
[18] U.S., *Statutes At Large*, Vol. 68, June 18, 1934, pp. 984-988.
[19] Proceedings of the meeting held by Senator Elmer Thomas and A. C. Monohan, Assistant to the Commissioner of Indian Affairs, with the Indians of the Kiowa Reservation relative to the Wheeler-Howard law, Anadarko, Oklahoma, October 23, 1934, pp. 4-13, RG 75, NA, Fort Worth Federal Records Center.
[20] Harold L. Ickes to Elmer Thomas, undated manuscript, RG 51 NA.
[21] Proceedings of the meeting held by Senator Elmer Thomas and A. C. Monohan, Assistant to the Commissioner of Indian Affairs, with the Indians of the Kiowa Reservation relative to the Wheeler-Howard law, Anadarko, Oklahoma, October 23, 1934, pp. 4-13, RG 75 NA, Fort Worth Federal Records Center.
[22] Philp, *John Collier's Crusade For Indian Reform*, pp. 177-179.
[23] House, Committee on Indian Affairs, *Hearings, On H.R. 6234, To Promote The General Welfare of the Indians of Oklahoma*, 74th Cong., 1st Sess., 1935, pp. 1-4.
[24] *Ibid.*
[25] *Ibid.*, p. 81; and House, Committee on Indian Affairs, *Hearings, On H.R. 7781, Indian Conditions and Affairs*, 74th Cong., 1st Sess., 1935, pp. 15-25.
[26] Consult the following newspapers for examples of newspaper opposition to the Thomas-Rogers Bill: "Indian Freedom Threatened," *Okmulgee Daily Times*, April 5, 1935; "Time for Heroic Action," *Muskogee Daily Phoenix*, April 6, 1935; and "New Bill Hailed as Dangerous to Oklahoma Indians," *Tulsa Daily World*, April 7, 1935.
[27] J. J. Howard to Elmer Thomas, March 16, 1935, Elmer Thomas Papers, WHC.
[28] House, Committee on Indian Affairs, *Hearings, on H.R. 6234, To Promote The General Welfare of Oklahoma Indians*, 74th Cong., 1st Sess., 1935, pp. 192-193.
[29] "Collier Argues for Thomas-Rogers Oklahoma Bill," *American Indian Defense Association Bulletin* XXII (April 8, 1935), pp. 1-4.
[30] Peter M. Wright, "John Collier and the Oklahoma Indian Welfare Act of 1936," *Chronicles of Oklahoma*, XL, No. 2 (Autumn, 1972), pp. 367-368.
[31] Theodore Haas, *Ten Years of Tribal Government Under IRA* (Washington, D.C.: U.S. Indian Service, 1947), pp. 43-45.
[32] Theodore W. Taylor, *The States and Their Indian Citizens* (Washington, D.C.: U.S. Department of the Interior, 1972), pp. 242-243.
[33] Haas, *Ten Years of Tribal Government Under IRA*, pp. 43-45.
[34] Angie Debo, *And Still The Waters Run* (Princeton, N. J.: Princeton University Press, 1940), pp. 377, 387.
[35] Angie Debo, *The Five Civilized Tribes of Oklahoma: Report on Social and Economic Conditions* (Philadelphia: Indian Rights Association, 1951), pp. 17-19.

[36] *Ibid.*; Expenditures for Resettlement Communities at Wilburton and McCurtain, Five Civilized Tribes Agency Jurisdiction to March 31, 1939, RG 48, NA, Central Files, 1937-1953.
[37] Harold L. Ickes to the President of the Senate, January 19, 1942, Central Files, 1937-1953, RG 48 NA.
[38] A. C. Cooley, Memorandum to Walter Woehlke, January 7, 1944, Central Files 1937-53, RG 48 NA.
[39] Walter V. Woehlke, Memorandum for the Solicitor, December 20, 1943, RG 48, NA, Central Files, 1937-1953; and Harold L. Ickes to the President of the Senate, January 19, 1942, Central Files, 1937-1953, RG 48 NA.
[40] Morris E. Opler, "The Creek Indian Towns of Oklahoma In 1937," in Harold N. Ottaway, ed., *Papers in Anthropology*, Vol. XIII (Spring 1972), pp. 3-9.
[41] John Collier to Elmer Thomas, July 26, 1938, Central Files, 1937-1953, RG 48 NA.
[42] Memorandum for the Commissioner of Indian Affairs (undated); Walter V. Woehlke, Memorandum for the Solicitor, December 29, 1943; and A. C. Cooley, Memorandum to Walter V. Woehlke, January 7, 1944, Central Files, 1937-1953, RG 48 NA.
[43] Debo, *The Five Civilized Tribes of Oklahoma*, pp. 4-7, 24-25.
[44] John Collier, Memorandum on S.B. 2206, April 21, 1939, Harold L. Ickes to Usher Burdick, April 26, 1939, Files on Bruner and the Oklahoma Racket, RG 75 NA.
[45] James H. Howard, "Pan-Indian Culture of Oklahoma," *Scientific Monthly*, LXXXI (November 1955), pp. 215-220; and Debo, *The Five Civilized Tribes of Oklahoma*, pp. 4-8.
[46] Undated newspaper clipping, "Full-blood Gives His View of the Wheeler-Howard bill, Elmer Thomas Papers, WHC.

Constitutions for the Indians

[1] Arrell M. Gibson, *Oklahoma, A History of Five Centuries* (Norman, Oklahoma: Harlow Publishing Corporation, 1965), Ernest Wallace, *Comanches, Lords of the South Plains* (Norman, Oklahoma: University of Okahoma, 1952), pp. 349-353. The Apaches in this article are sometimes referred to as the Kiowa-Apaches to distinguish them from the Apaches of New Mexico and Arizona.
[2] For numerous reports, correspondence, and newspaper clippings on Indian participation in county and regional fairs see File 6950-1923-100-Kiowa; Records of the Commissioner of Indian Affairs, RG 75 NA, Washington, D.C. For a description of federal policy in the Kiowa jurisdiction in the 1920s see "General Agency and Reservation Program now in use at the Kiowa Agency, 1929;" in the same file as above. This is a one hundred-page report written by the superintendent. For Craterville Indian fairs see Muriel H. Wright, "The American Indian Exposition," *The Chronicles of Oklahoma*, Vol. XXIV, No. 2 (Summer, 1946), pp. 158-165.
[3] Superintendent J. A. Buntin to A. C. Cooley, October 24, 1930; File 6950-1923-100-Kiowa; RG 75 NA.
[4] Florence Tibby (of Pittsburg, Pennsylvania) to the Secretary of Interior, Ray Wilbur, June 26, 1931; Florence Tibby to Commissioner of Indian Affairs Charles J. Rhoads, June 26, 1931; Rev. J. Clifford Mathews (of Birmingham, Michigan) to Rhoads, July 29, 1931; Mathews to Wilbur, July 29, 1931. See also Rev. John C. Slater (of Beaver Falls, Pennsylvania) to Rhoads, June 30, 1931; Rev. H. F. Gilbert (of Walters, Oklahoma) to Commissioner of Indian Affairs, May 22, 1931. Rev. Gilbert's letter was highly accusatory of Federal Indian policy. In his attempt to light a fire under Commissioner Rhoads and Superintendent Buntin he sent copies

of the letter to several people. The fire was soon burning brightly in many places. File 338-33-1931-062-Kiowa; RG 75 NA.

[5] Circular letter of Superintendent Buntin to "Friends" (calling for a Conference), dated November 6, 1931; File 338-33-1931-062-Kiowa; RG 75 NA.

[6] "Findings of Conference of Government Employees, Missionaries, and Indians at Anadarko Meeting," December 31, 1931; File 338-33-1931-062-Kiowa; RG 75 NA. And see also the "Proceedings" of the conference in the same file.

[7] The 1935 population was a follows: Kiowa, 2,170; Comanche, 2,130; Apache, 324; in *Annual Report of the Secretary of Interior for 1935* (Washington, D.C.: Government Printing Office, 1935), p. 165. For tribal government see Superintendent Walter McCown to Commissioner of Indian Affairs, July 31, 1934, enclosing "Questionaire on Tribal Government," p. 5, File 9623-A-1936-068-Kiowa. And see also the section on tribal government in the above cited "General Agency and Reservation Program Now in Use at the Kiowa Agency, 1929," File 6950-1923-100-Kiowa; RG 75 NA.

[8] "1932 Constitution of the Kiowa, Comanche, and Apache," enclosed in letter of McCown to Commissioner, July 31, 1934; File 9623-A-1936-068-Kiowa; RG 75 NA.

[9] McCown to Commissioner, July 31, 1934, with "Questionaire on Tribal Government," pp. 3, 5, 6; File 9623-1936-068-Kiowa; RG 75 NA.

[10] For an evaluation of Collier's developing ideas and program see Kenneth R. Philp, *John Collier's Crusade for Indian Reform, 1920-1954* (Tucson: University of Arizona Press, 1977), pp. 92-160.

[11] United States, *Statutes at Large*, Vol. 48, pt. 1, chapter 576, pp. 984-988 ("Indian Reorganization Act"); see especially, Section 13.

[12] United States Congress, House of Representative, Committee on Indian Affairs, *Hearings on H.R. 6234, A Bill to Promote the Welfare of the Indians of Oklahoma*; 74th Congress, 1st session; see pages 8-13 for Collier's statement, and also pp. 194-216; (Hearings in April, 1935); cited hereinafter as H.R., *1935 Hearings*, United States Congress, Senate, Committee On Indian Affairs, *Hearings on S. 2047, A Bill to Promote the Welfare of the Indians of Oklahoma*, 74th Cong., 1st Sess., pages 99-105, (Hearings in April, 1935).

[13] Largely because of eastern Oklahoma political interest the first version was considerably amended and differed from the final version as passed in 1936. The Indian probate clauses in the 1935 version caught especial fire from eastern Oklahoma. See the hearings cited in Footnote 12, and see also United States Congress, House of Representatives, Committee on Indian Affairs, *Hearings on S. 2047, A Bill to Promote the Welfare of the Indians of Oklahoma*, 74th Cong., 2nd Sess., pp. 6-51, (Hearings in April, 1936). The final act is United States *Statutes at Large*, Vol. 49, pt. 1, chapter 831, pp. 1967-1968 ("Oklahoma Indian Welfare Act").

[14] United States Congress, Senate, Subcommittee of the Committee on Indian Affairs, *Hearings on Survey of Conditions of the Indians*, Part 15, 71st Cong., 3rd Sess., November 17-20, 1930, pp. 7307-7311, 7374-7377, 7462-7466.

[15] H. R., *1935 Hearings*, pp. 8-13, 194-205, Senate, *1935 Hearings*, pp. 10-17.

[16] For a summary of the procedure see Field Agent Ben Dwight to Regional Coordinator A. C. Monahan, January 27, 1938, File 9623-1936-066-Kiowa, RG 75 NA.

[17] "1935 Constitution of Kiowa, Comanche, and Apache," File 9623-1936-066-Kiowa, RG 75 NA.

[18] Assistant Commissioner F. H. Daiker to Assistant Commissioner William Zimmerman, February 7, 1938, File 9623-1936-066-Kiowa, RG 75 NA.

[19] Dwight to McCown, May 14, 1937 (two letters); Dwight to Monahan January 27, 1938; File 9623-1936-066-Kiowa, RG 75 NA.

[20] Dwight to Monahan, January 29, 1938; File 9623-1936-066-Kiowa, RG 75 NA. The Apache voted a second time by a larger margin.

[21] *Ibid.*

[22] The Comanche and Apache 1937 Constitutions had similar provisions. A copy of the Kiowa Constitution is in File 9623-A-1936-068-Kiowa. Copies of the proposed 1937 Constitutions of the Comanche and Apache are in File 9509-A-1936-068-Kiowa, RG 75 NA.

[23] See File 9623-1936-067-Kiowa, RG 75 NA, for information on the Comanche cooperative. United States Congress, Senate, Sub-Committee of the Committee on Indian Affairs, *Hearings on a Survey of Conditions of the Indians*, Part 37, 76th Cong., 1st Sess. (Hearings in October, 1937), pp. 21290-21291. Sections 3 and 4 of the Thomas-Rogers Act deal with tribal government and cooperatives.

[24] Senate, *1937 Hearings*, p. 21290.

[25] *Ibid*, pp. 21287-21289. McCown to Commissioner of Indian Affairs, December 19, 1938; Dwight to Monahan, January 27, 1938, File 9623-1936-066-Kiowa, RG 75 NA.

[26] Dwight to Monahan, January 27, 1938; McCown to Commissioner of Indian Affairs, February 1, 1938; Daiker to Zimmerman, February 7, 1938; Monahan to McCown, December 12, 1938, File 9623-1936-066-Kiowa, RG 75 NA.

[27] Monahan to Commissioner of Indian Affairs, February 3, 1938; McCown to Commissioner of Indian Affairs, February 1, 1938; Monahan to McCown, December 12, 1938; "Resolution of Guy Quoetone and Others," December 14, 1938; Albert Attocknie to McCown, November 30, 1938, File 9623-1936-066-Kiowa, RG 75 NA.

[28] United States Congress, House, Committee on Indian Affairs, *Hearings on House Joint Resolution 290, Kiowa Commanche and Apache Indians Jurisdictional Act*, 76th Cong., 1st Sess., Hearings on July 18 and 21, 1939, pp. 5-21, 35-45.

[29] Zimmerman to McCown, May 6, 1940; Zimmerman to McCown, July 12, 1940, File 9623-1936-066-Kiowa; Erma O. Hicks to Tribal Relations Memoranda, March 24, 1947, File 9623-A-1936-068-Kiowa, RG 75 NA.

[30] The references in Footnote 29 apply; and see also Attocknie to Congressman Jed Johnson, April 29, 1940; Senator Elmer Thomas to Commissioner John Collier, April 5, 1940, File 9623-1936-066-Kiowa, RG 75 NA.

[31] Proceedings of the General Council of the Kiowa, Comanche and Apache Indians held at the Riverside Indian School on Thursday, October 10, 1940; "1940 Constitution of the Kiowa, Comanche and Apache Tribal Business Committee," File 9623-1936-066-Kiowa, RG 75 NA.

Index

— A —

— B —

— C —

— D —

— E —

— F —

— G —

— H —

— I —

— J —

— K —

— L —

— M —

— N —

— O —

— P —

— Q —

— R —

— S —

— T —

— U —

— V —

— W —

— Y —